Happy Mother's Day '09

TO A MOTHER AS BEAUTIFUL
AS THE GARDENS OF CAPE COD!

WE LOVE YOU!

ROB, WENDY, EMILY, WILL + ANNA
XO     XO        XO        XO         XO

A Garden Lover's Cape Cod

# A GARDEN LOVER'S
# CAPE COD

## C.L. FORNARI

COMMONWEALTH EDITIONS

*Beverly, Massachusetts*

ISBN-13: 978-1-933212-34-0
ISBN-10: 1-933212-34-9

Library of Congress Cataloging-in-Publication Data

Fornari, C.L. (Cynthia Lynn), 1950–
A garden lover's Cape Cod / C.L. Fornari.
p. cm.
ISBN 1-933212-34-9 (alk. paper)
1. Gardens—Massachusetts—Cape Cod.  I. Title.

SB451.34.M4F67 2007
712'.60974492—dc22

Cover design by John Barnett / 4 Eyes Design
Interior design by Gary G. Gore
Printed in China

Published by Commonwealth Editions, an imprint of Memoirs Unlimited, Inc.,
266 Cabot Street, Beverly, Massachusetts 01915.

Visit our Web site: www.commonwealtheditions.com.

Visit C.L. Fornari on the Web at www.gardenlady.com.

10  9  8  7  6  5  4  3  2

*This book is dedicated*
*to the gardeners of Cape Cod.*
*You make this lovely region an*
*even more beautiful place.*

# CONTENTS

# ACKNOWLEDGMENTS

I am, of course, most thankful to all who so generously invited me into their gardens, or graciously said, "Yes," when I left them notes or knocked on their doors. I don't know if kind people are attracted to gardening, or if the act of tending plants somehow encourages bigheartedness, but I am genuinely grateful to all of you for your willingness to share your gardens with others.

Thanks to Will Clarke of Perennial Solutions, Tim Acton of Tim Acton Landscaping, and Jeanie Gillis, horticulturist at Heritage Museums and Gardens, for helping me during the height of their professional seasons. Mike Wright was kind enough to steer me to some Provincetown jewels, and Roberta Clark of the Cooperative Extension was always available and helpful when I needed her expertise.

I am grateful to Webster Bull and the staff of Commonwealth Editions for sharing my vision, and to Ann Twombly for pulling the weeds out of the manuscript. As always, I'm extremely thankful that my husband, Dan Fornari, is both supportive of this project and tolerant of my general plant-mania.

Finally, I'm so appreciative of the Master Gardeners of Barnstable County, those who volunteer in our parks and gardens, and all the Cape Cod garden clubs. The members of these organizations are tireless horticultural volunteers who improve our landscape *and* our enjoyment of everyday life: I applaud you all.

# INTRODUCTION

When I first moved to Cape Cod and began talking with other gardeners, I heard the same comment again and again: "Gardening is really different here!" People would mention the wind, the typically cold spring season, and the difficulty of planting in sand. And yet, despite these challenges, as I traveled from Woods Hole to Provincetown, I saw beautiful, flourishing gardens.

As I tended my own Cape Cod landscape I learned that in the right circumstances, the wind encourages plants to grow tough and strong. I discovered that although spring can be chilly and damp, the mild fall weather often lasts through Thanksgiving. And the sandy soil? Given regular applications of compost or other organic matter, the sand guarantees the excellent drainage that so many plants require.

I learned that our ocean-moderated temperatures are perfect for growing a wide range of plants, including the much-loved roses and blue hydrangeas. And looking beyond the growing conditions and the plants that thrive in them, I found enthusiastic gardeners creating lovely landscapes.

We are drawn to Cape Cod because of the ocean, the sea breeze, and the New England character of our towns and villages. It is an area that reminds us of childhood summer vacations and the pleasures of being outdoors. So it's natural, I suppose, that many view their land-

scapes as an extension of their homes, and they choose beautiful plantings and ornaments to enhance these "outdoor rooms."

The types of gardens found on the Cape are as varied as the population. English perennial borders, wildflower meadows, Japanese designs, and rose gardens all flourish here. But the style that predominates, and perhaps is most appropriate to this region, is an informal blend of all types of plants: trees, shrubs, perennials, and annuals. Added to the plants is a multiplicity of structures and ornaments that add solidity and charm. As you look from garden to garden, it is clear that these plants and objects are combined in unique ways. Equally apparent is the obvious pleasure that people find in their landscapes.

Beyond the private gardens, I've been delighted at the number of Cape properties that are open to the public. Ranging from the manifestation of one person's vision to the product of many devoted volunteers, the parks and gardens of Cape Cod are lively and diverse.

*A Garden Lover's Cape Cod* is a tour of some of this region's very special landscapes. It is a reminder of the many public treasures that are just a short drive away, and it allows a rare peek through the hedge at some of the loveliest private gardens in the area. And most important, it is celebration of the gardeners who make the beauty of the land a suitable match for the splendor of the sea.

# Chapter 1

# PARKS AND GARDENS

Cape Cod's denizens are particularly blessed; we truly have the best of many worlds. Surrounded on all sides by water, we enjoy beautiful vistas and a refreshing sea breeze. Our interior is filled with lakes and kettle ponds. On the whole, the ground we plant in may seem to be straight off the beach, but an amazing amount of vegetation thrives in these sandy soils. There are woodlands, marshes, and fields that are preserved for the public to enjoy, and there are also many beautiful gardens that are available to all.

Gardens and wild spaces derive much of their beauty from the plants that grow in them, but a cultivated garden differs from a natural area in that people are involved with the choosing and arrangement of the plants. Every garden, then, contains a great deal of the gardener along with the plants. A garden is a group partnership between the place, the plants, and the people who design and maintain it.

Most of the public gardens on the Cape started with someone who had a private vision or passion, and now these gardens continue to exist through the efforts of non-profit organizations and dedicated volunteers. Each of the gardens pictured here has its own unique style and a spirit that has been determined by the site, the plants chosen, and the objects and buildings that complement the landscape.

All these gardens are resources for learning about plants and gardening. Even for non-gardeners, wandering through such lovely landscapes is a prescription for a rejuvenating day out. Cape Cod's open gardens are truly filled with beauty, information, and inspiration for everyone to enjoy.

*Leucothoe* and rhododendrons bloom along the roadway at Heritage, and the daylily foliage softens sections of a stone wall.

## A Park on the Pond

As we drive up Fells Road in Falmouth, the large trees that overhang and frame the drive, and roadside plantings in front of the homes along the street, create a lush, woodsy atmosphere even before we arrive at Spohr Garden. Without fanfare the parking area appears on the left; across the road is the path to the gardens. This unassuming entry is appropriate for these informally planted woodlands; even before the car is parked the tone is set for a relaxing stroll through shady gardens.

Spohr Garden was created by Margaret and Charles D. Spohr in the 1950s, and for more than forty years they generously shared the plantings around their home with the public. Although Charles Spohr died in 1997, and Margaret Spohr passed away in the spring of 2001, these public gardens continue to be the site of picnics, small weddings, and countless walks.

Located on six acres on Oyster Pond, Spohr Garden is most noted for the spring daffodil display, when hundreds of thousands of daffodils carpet the area. Brilliant color from the large rhododendrons follows the spring bulb display, and the area across the road contains a sunnier garden where daylilies and other perennials bloom through the summer.

Throughout the property a collection of large millstones and ships' bells provide a wonderful solidity that balances the texture of the green foliage. Charles Spohr also collected large ships' anchors, and these are placed in the gardens and along the water's edge, displayed against the sparkling background of the pond.

▲ Spohr Garden, in Falmouth, is delightful all summer, but it is dazzling in early spring. Thousands of yellow daffodils make an impressive display next to the shining blue of Oyster Pond.

◄◄ In addition to the huge daffodil beds, Spohr Garden is filled with drifts of Siberian squill (*Scilla siberica*) and rhododendrons, and, in other sections of the property, large groups of a lesser-known evergreen, *Skimmia japonica*. *Skimmia* are dense and low growing, with dark green leaves. Female *Skimmia* have bright red berries in winter months, and plants of both sexes prefer the dappled shade of Spohr Garden's open woodland.

◄ One of the many ships' anchors in Charles Spohr's collection rises above large groups of daffodils.

▲▲ In June large drifts of ragged robin *(Lychnis flos-cuculi)* and oxeye daisies *(Chrysanthemum leucanthemum)* fill the wildflower garden at Green Briar Nature Center.
▲ The vintage-style jam kitchen at the Green Briar Nature Center sits ready to process many pots of bubbling fruit.

▲ A true wildflower garden is not for those who demand that every plant be grown in its own separate space. Wildflowers travel and mingle, growing in communities of plants instead of individual clumps. Here the pink-flowering ragged robin *(Lychnis flos-cuculi)* grows among the lush green foliage of plants that will bloom later in the season.

Meadow beauty *(Rhexia virginica)* is also known by the charming but somewhat puzzling name of "handsome Harry." This short wildflower is native to North America, and it blooms in July.

Crocosmia 'Lucifer' and tiger lilies *(Lilium lancifolium)* bloom red and orange in front of pale pink obedient plant *(Physostegia virginiana)* in the July wildflower garden at Green Briar.

The Spohr Charitable Trust is currently managing the gardens, and they are maintained with the help of several devoted volunteers.

## Going Wild

Garden lovers have the opportunity to walk on the wild side in Sandwich and in Brewster. In these Cape towns are wildflower gardens that celebrate untamed beauty and educate visitors about the diverse plant life outside the cultivated flowerbed.

### Green Briar Nature Center Wildflower Gardens

Wildflowers from all over the world grow along with Cape Cod native plants in the Green Briar gardens in Sandwich. These gardens cover a locust-shaded embankment, a sun-drenched meadow, and a wetland in front of a home built in 1780. These natural plantings have been planned and tended by Shirley Cross, a botanist who has also written a guide to the many plants growing in the gardens.

Since they are, after all, wild, these plants are allowed to self-seed and spread as they will, but that doesn't mean that the garden is untended. If a weed is any plant that is growing where you don't want it to be, any and every plant has the capacity to be weedy. And given the chance, weeds will invade any garden, even a garden that is planted with other weeds. So a committed group of volunteers keeps the undesirables out.

Greenbriar also houses a library and a jam kitchen. The Robert S. Swain Natural History Library has a collection of books and periodicals on the natural history of eastern Massachusetts. The jam kitchen is a living museum where visitors can see how garden produce is turned into jams, jellies, pickles, and relishes. The kitchen where these mouthwatering treats are prepared is similar to the one where Ida Putnam made the first preserves at Green Briar in 1903, and the sun-cooked preserves are made in the oldest commercial solar-cooking operation in the United States.

Also part of Green Briar is the Nature Center, run by the Thornton W. Burgess Society, located on Discovery Hill Road in Sandwich. When Thornton Burgess was young, one of his employers lived on this country road, and the area became the setting for many of Burgess's children's stories.

Next to the wildflower garden, where more than three hundred plants are labeled, are trails through the fifty-seven-acre Briar Patch Conservation area, which is the home of Peter Rabbit and other Thornton Burgess animal characters.

*Lyn Peabody Wildflower Garden*

Located next to the Cape Cod Museum of Natural History in Brewster is the Lyn Peabody Wildflower Garden. These woodland gardens were conceived when five members of the Nauset Garden Club began to plan the garden in 1985. The land, then a tangle of vines, brush, and invasive plants, was cleared in 1988. Today the garden is a testament to what happens when a group of enthusiastic gardeners decides to create something beautiful.

Lyn Peabody was one of the original members of this group, and she worked hard for the garden even as she battled breast cancer. After her death, it was decided that the new wildflower garden would bear her name.

Once the land was cleared and the soil prepared, garden club members began donating appropriate plants. Other plantings were purchased from Garden in the Woods, in Framingham, Massachusetts, which is maintained by the New England Wild Flower Society.

Although wildflowers usually thrive without being pampered, care had to be taken to provide all the specimens with the growing conditions they prefer. Newly placed plants need to be watered as they are getting established, and the entire garden needs to be kept free of vigorous ex-

◄ Mulched paths wind through the Green Briar wildflower gardens. The drifts of June-flowering perennials stretch along the walk near a multi-stemmed kousa dogwood.

▲ Wildflowers grow so enthusiastically in this Brewster garden that they advertise themselves. Mullein, oxeye daisies, and Queen Anne's lace threaten to cover the sign at the entrance to the garden.

► A path winds through a shady, fern-lined garden next to the Museum of Natural History in Brewster. At its most colorful in May, the Lyn Peabody Wildflower Garden was developed by plant enthusiasts from the Nauset Garden Club. The club continues the maintenance of this delightful garden.

# Native Perennials for Cape Cod Gardens

## Indigenous Plants for Full or Part Sun

Joe-pye weed (*Eupatorium purpureum*)—This *Eupatorium* is a tall, back-of-the-garden plant that blooms mauve-pink in mid- to late summer. Although in the wild it grows in moist ditches, this perennial tolerates average garden soil in full or part sun.

Goldenrod (*Solidago* species and hybrids)—A worthy garden perennial, goldenrod is often falsely accused of causing hay fever. In reality, the showy flowers of goldenrod are in bloom at the same time as the insignificant-looking flowers of ragweed, so the goldenrod gets the blame. Goldenrod is a problem-free, late-summer bloomer that makes a good cut flower. Various species and named cultivars are available, and this plant does best when not overfertilized.

Asters—From the tall New England aster (*Symphyotrichum novae-angliae*, syn. *Aster novae-angliae*) to the short aster 'Woods Blue', these perennials are butterfly magnets and one of the best plants for fall flower color. The lower stems of the tall asters are often bare, but they can be either sheared in May (cut three inches off the top of the plant with scissors) or planted behind midsize shrubs or perennials that will hide the lower part of the plant. Most asters spread when they are happy, so they'll need to be edited out periodically to keep them from taking over the garden.

Coreopsis (*C. grandiflora* and *C. verticillata*)—These yellow-flowering perennials are drought-tolerant and long-blooming. *C. grandiflora* often self-seeds, making it a good choice for a wildflower meadow. The fine foliage of *C. verticillata* complements the small flowers that appear all summer; the variety called 'Moonbeam' is especially popular for its long season of bloom and butter-yellow flowers. Because it can spread or self-seed, coreopsis needs to be divided or edited out of the garden every spring. *C. grandiflora* is in bloom in June, and *C. verticillata* from late June into August.

Coneflower (*Echinacea purpurea*)—From the species *E. purpurea* to the hybrids and cultivars such as 'Magnus', 'White Swan', and 'Sundown', there is an echinacea for every sunny garden. They are all long-blooming and drought-tolerant, and the central cones are attractive well into the fall. This native perennial attracts butterflies when they are in flower, and birds eat the seeds in the fall.

## Native Plants for Shade

Lady fern (*Athyrium filix-femina*)—Unlike some ferns that spread around the garden, these are clumping ferns that grow three feet high and four feet wide. This fern does well with once-a-week watering, but it will develop more quickly in damp soils. Lady ferns are easy to grow, and they are beautiful in the shade garden or used as greenery in cut-flower arrangements.

Goat's beard (*Aruncus dioicus*)—*Aruncus* is a large, dramatic plant for part shade and moist soil. Growing 4 to 6 feet tall and wide, goat's beard has feathery, cream-colored flowers in early summer. It is a good background or back-of-the-border plant that blooms best with at least three hours of direct sun.

Virginia bluebells (*Mertensia virginica*)—A treasure in the early spring, Virginia bluebells emerge from the soil in March with purple foliage. Leaves turn light green as the true-blue flowers emerge, and shortly after flowering the entire plant yellows and becomes dormant for the rest of the summer. A clump of *Mertensia* will grow larger, and the plant usually self-seeds in the garden as well. Virginia bluebells do well in organically rich soil in part sun or part shade.

Turtlehead (*Chelone glabra* and *C. oblique*)—White and pink turtleheads bloom in August and prefer to grow in slightly moist soil that has been well amended with organic matter. This 3-foot perennial thrives in part shade and bears some resemblance to snapdragons, to which it is related. Turtlehead is a reliable perennial that is completely carefree from spring to fall.

otic and invasive plants that continually threaten to take over. Members of the Nauset Garden Club take charge of the ongoing care of this lovely and educational retreat.

The Lyn Peabody Wildflower Garden is most striking in May, but flowers come into bloom from spring through late summer, and the walk in the shade of the surrounding trees is a treat throughout the season. Native lady's slipper orchids, jack-in-the-pulpits, and a fern collection are just a few of the plantings in this delightful garden.

## An Oasis in Osterville

Garden lovers who want to picnic in the company of unusual trees should make their way to Armstrong-Kelley Park in Osterville. This eight-acre property has been planted and maintained by the Cape Cod Horticultural Society for more than seventy years, and it boasts of flowers in bloom 365 days a year.

Community involvement is one of the special aspects of this park. Every kindergartner from the Osterville elementary school can plant daffodil bulbs in the garden and return for years afterward to enjoy them when they bloom.

Trails lead through naturalized woodland, rhododendrons, and hollies. There is a test area where gardeners can view some of the newer plants that are coming onto the market, and flowerbeds planted with annuals and perennials ring the lawn and picnic area. A wooden walkway makes it easy to view the water garden, and young children love the boardwalk that leads to a wooden train, into which they can climb and ring the bell.

What makes Armstrong-Kelley Park unique is the large collection of unusual mature trees. Magnolias, a weeping Atlantic cedar, and a large Franklinia are just a few of the beautiful specimen plantings.

## A Proud Heritage

The largest garden that is open to the public is just a short drive from the millpond in the center of Sandwich. With over seventy acres of gardens and mature trees, Heritage Museums and Gardens is a gardener's dream. It is also, perhaps, a testament to the healing aspects of tending plants.

Charles Owen Dexter bought the land that is now Heritage Museums and Gardens in 1921. At age fifty-nine he had been told that he didn't have long to live, so he retired to Sandwich and began working in the garden and hybridizing plants. In the subsequent twenty-two years that he lived, Charles Dexter developed between 150,000 and 200,000 new rhododendrons. He planted many of these on his property, which borders Shawme Pond, and gave others to nurseries, gardeners, and private botanical collections.

Many of these Dexter hybrids still grew on the estate

The spring display at Armstrong-Kelley Park includes hundreds of daffodils, many planted by the students at Osterville Elementary School. Starting with the star magnolia, several spring-flowering trees greet park visitors.

Forget-me-nots and sweet woodruff bloom alongside fading daffodils next to the Child's Garden of Verses boardwalk at Armstrong-Kelley Park in Osterville. Lined with poems that are placed on some of the fence posts, this walkway invites adults and children to pause in the shade and read a verse. The boardwalk leads to a wooden train sculpture where small children can "come aboard."

## Indigenous Shrubs for Cape Cod Gardens

Beach plum (*Prunus maritima*) is an attractive large shrub that can take on a windblown, sculptured look. Beach plums spread by suckering, forming multistemmed clumps that grow 4 to 8 feet high. Planting three or more in a group helps ensure cross-pollination and fruit production, but even when planted in groups, it is typical for beach plums to bear heavily one year and lightly the next.

Inkberry holly (*Ilex glabra*) is a lovely, loose shrub with lustrous, evergreen leaves. Inkberry tolerates part shade and average garden moisture, but it prefers full sun and slightly moist soil. Many cultivars are available that keep a lower, more compact form, so for foundation plantings or small gardens, varieties such as 'Compacta' and Nordic ('Chamzin') should be purchased. When inkberry is pruned regularly from the start, the foliage remains on the lower stems for a longer period.

Summersweet (*Clethra alnifolia*) perfumes the local woodland with its sweet scent, coming into bloom in late July or early August. In addition to the white or pink bottlebrush flowers, *Clethra* has beautiful fall color, and it is especially striking when planted where it will catch the evening sun in autumn. Plant summersweet in full sun to part shade, amending the soil well with compost or peat moss. Most *Clethra* grows 6 to 8 feet tall, but 'Hummingbird' is a cultivar that grows only 4 feet high.

Swamp azalea (*Rhododendron viscosum*), as its rather off-putting name suggests, does well in moist soils, but it will also thrive in normal garden conditions in part shade. Growing to about 8 feet high, this rhododendron blooms in early summer and the white flowers are extremely fragrant. Named cultivars of this plant include the July-blooming 'Lemon Drop', which has pale yellow, sweetly scented flowers.

Oakleaf hydrangea (*Hydrangea quercifolia*) is another native shrub that is valued for its flowers and the bright fall

when Mr. and Mrs. J.K. Lilly III purchased the property in the 1960s. The Lilly family opened Heritage Plantation of Sandwich to the public to display the Lilly collections of art, antique automobiles, and historical items. Also preserved for everyone's enjoyment were the rhododendrons, the parklike atmosphere, and many specimen trees.

Today gardeners and nongardeners alike enjoy these same rhododendrons, other mature shrubs and trees, and the diverse gardens on the property. The large hosta and daylily collections at Heritage are especially popular. Both curve around large lawns and contain numerous named species and cultivars. More than nine hundred daylilies bloom from July into August, and many visitors are surprised to see how many hosta varieties thrive in gardens that are located in full sun.

Equally informative, and extremely imaginative, is the new vine maze. Unlike a traditional maze of sheared shrubbery, the maze at Heritage was designed by Stephen Stimson to feature an attractive system of stainless steel vine supports along with rows of upright junipers and arborvitaes. Growing up the wire screening is a collection of annual and perennial vines, including morning glories, clematis, honeysuckle, climbing hydrangeas, and old-fashioned Dutchman's pipe.

As the vines fill in, other sections of the maze are visible through the metal screening, but that doesn't make the course any less confusing. As you walk through the maze, it is still possible to end up in a dead end if you aren't careful. Informational signage and the appeal of so many different vines make the experience enjoyable and educational, even when you find yourself in a blind alley.

In addition to the maze, Heritage also has a labyrinth. A labyrinth is often confused with a maze, but labyrinths are not intended to confuse or disorient those who enter. Walk-

---

color of its foliage. Oakleaf hydrangeas form flower buds the year before blooming, so they shouldn't be pruned except to remove deadwood or oddly shaped branches. This hydrangea can grow 6 feet high and wide, but if a smaller size is needed, the variety 'Pee Wee' does not grow much more than 3 feet high. *Hydrangea quercifolia* grows well in sun or part shade.

Bayberry (*Myrica pensylvanica*) is a nitrogen-fixing, deciduous shrub that grows in rich or poor soils. Spreading by suckering, a bayberry can form a large colony over time and is a good plant for stretches of sand, informal shrub borders, or slopes that need stabilizing. Plant bayberry in full or part sun. This shrub will tolerate coastal or other exposed locations, and it may be periodically pruned to the ground to control size or renew growth.

Bearberry (*Arctostaphylos uva-ursi*) is a low, handsome evergreen plant that can grow in pure sand. Large patches can be seen growing on sand dunes and the dry banks along highways, but it is also a good groundcover for the landscape. Bearberry grows between 4 and 8 inches tall, depending on the variety. It is best to purchase bearberry in nursery-grown pots, as it is extremely difficult to root or transplant. Although newly planted bearberry should be watered weekly, once this plant is established it resents frequent sprinklings, so plant it in areas where there is no supplemental irrigation. Bearberry grows well in dry soils and looks attractive when planted with sedum, ornamental grasses, and other drought-tolerant plants.

'Henry's Garnet' Itea (*Itea virginica* 'Henry's Garnet') is a wonderful form of our native Virginia sweetspire. This *Itea* is a deciduous shrub that grows 3 to 4 feet high and spreads slowly in average garden soil. Drooping white bottlebrush flowers cover the plant in June, and the foliage holds its burgundy-red fall color for more than two months. *Itea* will grow faster and larger in wet soils, but it tolerates regular garden sites that are watered weekly. 'Henry's Garnet' is a good shrub for wet locations, foundation plantings, and the front layer of mixed-shrub borders.

ing a labyrinth is a form of meditation: the layout forces you to circle your way toward the labyrinth's center and out again, as you calm your thoughts and move toward your own center.

The labyrinth at Heritage is located in the shade of tall trees, and they seem to stand witness, their stateliness creating a soothing and serious atmosphere above the clamshell pathways. Marty Cain, who has created many labyrinths around the world, designed this simple, peaceful construction.

Heritage also has an herb garden, heath and heather collection, holly dell, annual and perennial gardens, and many colorful containers. This lovely property is a special part of the Cape that repeatedly draws garden lovers back.

A cheerful mix of annuals and perennials surrounds the sign by the entry to Heritage Museums and Gardens in Sandwich.

Rhododendrons weighed down with flowers make the path to the vine maze seem like the entrance to a secret garden.

◀ Because most of us live on small properties, we don't usually have the pleasure of walking through a large grove of tall trees. In wild areas the trees might be mature, but the untamed underbrush forces us to stay out or to stick to established paths. Such natural areas exist at Heritage, but there are also stands of trees that rise above low grass, allowing us to see the open fields beyond and giving us a vantage point from which to appreciate the textures of the tree trunks.

▼ Large, extravagant rhododendron flowers make a spectacular display in the late spring and early summer. Many of the Dexter hybrid rhodies were selected for fragrance as well as color, so a walk through Heritage in May and early June is both a visual and an aromatic experience.

White camellia-like flowers dot the dark green foliage on this Japanese _Stewartia (Stewartia pseudocamellia)_, a tree prized for its midsummer bloom and multicolored, exfoliating bark. Visitors to Heritage are delighted by the way whole flowers drop to the ground, making the area near the carousel look as if there's just been a wedding or flower festival.

◀ The hosta collection forms a tapestry of color and texture in this large perennial garden. Located in front of a large windmill, this garden demonstrates that many varieties of hosta are very sun-tolerant, and they combine nicely with the astilbe, *Eupatorium,* and other perennials that come into bloom later in the summer.

▼ The collection of daylilies stretches around one of Heritage's vast lawns. Daylilies begin blooming in late June and thereafter provide a succession of summer color as early-, mid-, and late-season varieties come into flower.

▶ Early morning dew gives the daylily blossoms a jewellike appearance. Daylilies in Heritage's collection are all labeled so that visitors can make lists of those they might like to plant in their own gardens.

▶▶ The entry garden at Heritage is a cheerful mix of hydrangeas, delphiniums, dahlias, *Agastache*, yellow rudbeckia, and petunias. This blend of shrubs, perennials, and annuals was designed and planted by Michael P. Neath, and the colorful beds greet visitors to Heritage as they enter the main parking lot.

▶▶▶ Walking a labyrinth is a form of meditation, and where better to look for such a calming journey than among stately trees? Marty Cain, one of the best-known labyrinth designers in North America, planned this peaceful oasis that is outlined in cobblestones, paved with crushed clamshells, and embraced by majestic trees.

▼ The Hart Family Vine Maze is a recent addition to the Heritage collection of gardens. Designed by Stephen Stimson of Stephen Stimson Associates, this unusual maze is intriguing, entertaining, and informative. Children enjoy traveling through and solving the puzzle of how to get from beginning to end, and signs throughout the maze provide information about nature and plants. Adults, too, appreciate the educational information, and they can instantly see a living catalog of annual and perennial vines.

▼ The sprawling fringe tree *(Chionanthus virginicus)* is a favorite with those who visit Heritage in June. The fragrant white flowers and the fresh, new foliage seem to float around trailing branches that fill the circle near the administration building.

# Heavenly at Heritage

Twelve of the most popular plants at Heritage Museums and Gardens:

Dexter rhododendrons—The rhododendrons bred by Charles Dexter are some of the best flowering shrubs for the Middle Atlantic region. Visitors to Heritage are in awe of their clear colors and the size of the blooms, and varieties such as 'Spice' and 'Honeydew' are prized for their fragrance as well as their striking appearance when in bloom. The Dexter hybrid called 'Scintillation' is one of the most requested plants at rhododendron nurseries.

Catmint—The long row of giant catmint (*Nepeta faassenii* × 'Six Hills Giant') at the entrance to Heritage draws comments from visitors every June. This large *Nepeta* blooms prolifically in early summer, and if kept deadheaded will flower sporadically the rest of the season. All catmints appreciate full sun and good drainage, and they can be cut to the ground after bloom if desired.

English holly—Although English holly (*Ilex aquifolium*) is slow-growing, over time it will become a large tree. Heritage has some outstanding examples of these mature hollies. The bright red berries on the female plants show well against the dark green, shiny leaves. This holly grows well in sandy loam and prefers a part-sun, slightly sheltered location.

*Franklinia*—Named for Benjamin Franklin, this tree is thought to be extinct in the wild. Two eighteenth-century botanists, John and William Bartram, found a small stand of these trees in the wilds of coastal Georgia in 1765. That group of *Franklinia*, or Franklin tree, is now gone and it is speculated that all *Franklinia alatamaha* now under cultivation are descendents of those trees. *Franklinia* blooms in the late summer into early fall, and it is frequently seen as a multistemmed small tree. Because it needs good drainage, it grows well in the sandy soils on Cape Cod, so long as the area is well amended with compost and peat moss.

Fringe tree—When Heritage's fringe tree (*Chionanthus virginicus*) is in bloom, people fall in love. The lacy white blossoms form a cloud of fragrant flowers in late May or early June, and its often-asymmetrical form just adds to its charm. Fringe trees are relatively slow-growing, eventually reaching 12 to 20 feet high and wide. In addition to the fine flowers, the fruit on this native tree is attractive to birds.

Shadbush or Serviceberry—One of the first trees to bloom in the spring, shadbush (*Amelanchier canadensis*) is covered with billowy masses of flowers well before the leaves are out on most deciduous trees. Often seen as a multistemmed or low-branching specimen, shadbush thrives in full sun or part shade, often growing to around 25 feet high. Shadbush is also called shadblow, both names coming from the fact that it blooms, and the petals *blow*, when the shad fish swim upstream. The name serviceberry comes from the usefulness of the berries, which at one time were commonly used to make preserves and pies. Anyone who wants to use *Amelanchier* fruit will have to get to it before the wildlife, however: the berries are also a favorite of birds.

Star magnolia—Another early-blooming small tree that is in flower before the foliage breaks dormancy, *Magnolia stellata* is a bushy, densely foliaged small tree that grows to about 20 feet high. It is most commonly seen with white flowers, but it's available in varieties that have pink blossoms as well. The flower buds that form in the end of the summer, and the structure of the branches, make this tree attractive over the winter.

Flame azaleas—The flame azalea (*Rhododendron calendulaceum*) is a deciduous shrub that grows quite large. It makes a fine specimen plant, and it combines well in mixed shrub borders and naturalized privacy screens. Loose clusters of spring flowers are bright colors, yellow, orange, pink, or red. This variety of azalea does well in full sun, but it requires a moist soil that is rich in organic matter.

Umbrella pine—One of the classiest evergreens on Cape Cod, umbrella pine (*Sciadopitys verticillata*) has thick, dark green, glossy needles that radiate out in whorls from the stems. Because this tree grows 20 to 30 feet high and 20 feet wide, care should be taken not to plant it too close to a building or another tree. The cones are ornamental, and the umbrella pine is a stately, problem-free plant in the landscape.

Mayflower viburnum—Also called Korean spice viburnum (*Viburnum carlesii*), this shrub has pink buds in early

One of the pleasures of walking through Heritage Museums and Gardens is seeing shrubs and trees that have been allowed to grow to their full size and natural shape. Although throughout the grounds there are yews that have been sheared into topiary shapes, there are also banks of rhododendrons and specimen trees such as this weeping spruce (*Picea abies* 'Pendula') that have not been pruned back in an attempt to keep them small.

spring that open to highly fragrant white flowers in May. The foliage on this medium-sized shrub can be textured, and the leaves turn bright red in the fall. Korean spice viburnum grows well in full sun to part shade, and it can grow between 5 and 8 feet tall.

Weeping spruce—This spectacular specimen tree is fairly fast-growing and has an upright central trunk, especially when trained against a pole as a young plant. Weeping spruce (*Picea abies* 'Pendula') grows to 30 feet high and 20 feet wide, however, so it should not be planted too close to walkways or buildings.

Witch hazel—There are several species of this large shrub, including the native Virginia witch hazel (*Hamamelis virginiana*), which blooms in the fall, and the Chinese and Japanese forms (*H. mollis* and *H. japonica*) and hybrids that bloom in late winter. The Chinese witch hazel is the most fragrant, but the hybrids such as 'Arnold Promise' have the showiest flowers. Witch hazel is a problem-free plant that looks good in mixed-shrub borders, as a background plant, or as a specimen shrub in open areas.

# Chapter 2

# CAPE COD TREASURES

## The View from the Street

**W**hen you drive along Cape Cod roadways, it is obvious that this region is filled with plant lovers. *From the landscapes planted with a few gorgeous specimen trees to the properties where the owner has gone crazy for roses or hydrangeas, this area*

is filled with intriguing gardens and the people who create them. Happily, many of these gardens are either open to the public or visible from the road.

Gardeners tend to be a generous group of people, and a number of them choose to share the results of their labor with others. For some this means creating flower gardens in the front yard so that those who walk or drive by can enjoy their handiwork. Placing perennial borders and other beds in front of the house is contrary to traditional American landscaping. Conventional properties feature foundation plantings around the house, lawn and trees between the house and the street, and flower and vegetable gardens in the backyard.

Locating gardens where they are visible to passersby benefits everyone, but the placement may not be instigated by altruism. Because plants can be particular about their growing conditions, the position of a garden is often a practical matter. If the sunniest area on the property happens to be in front of the house, than that's where the roses and flower borders need to be.

Other functional considerations might also dictate the choice of front-yard plants. There might be an area that is

The largest field at the Cape Cod Lavender Farm is at the top of the hill. Most of the lavender grown at the farm is either 'Hidcote' or 'Munstead', two varieties that are especially hardy on Cape Cod.

21

▲▲ At the Olde Cottage Garden the beds are kept weed-free, whereas some self-sowing plants, such as the pale pink penstemon, are allowed to wander in selected areas. This group of wild and tame is one of the charms of the gardens designed by Jeffrey Thomas.

▲◄ A stash of small terra-cotta pots fills an old wooden crate on the porch of Coco Plum Garden Antiques in Sandwich.

▲ Along Route 6A dozens of antiques stores offer treasures for the garden. An old wheelbarrow announces when Coco Plum is open.

Many Cape Cod businesses know that a flower garden adds tremendous appeal to a storefront. Roses, perennials, and blue fescue grass decorate the entrance of Pastiche in Barnstable, and this Provincetown building, home to Cape and Island Travel and Peter Karl Real Estate, is about as flower-packed with annuals as one small building can be.

John Nemec tends the ever-changing gardens in front of his parents' home and business in Barnstable. In this bed he planted a colorful mix of annuals and perennials.

An old wooden chair becomes a charming planter at Odile, a clothing store on Route 28.

Ed Nemec says that he frequently sees cars slow when they pass the gardens his son planted. He reports that one man even stopped to ask if he could pick a bouquet for his wife!

'New Dawn' and 'Blaze' climbing roses cover the fence around a cottage garden at the Hopkins House Bakery Shop in Brewster.

Cape Cod is filled with garden businesses. From the farm stands that sell locally grown plants and produce to the large, full-service garden centers, there are treasures to be found from one end of the Cape to the other. Crow Farm, on Route 6A in Sandwich, is the picture of a Cape Cod country farm stand.

▲ It's spring along Route 6A: purple creeping phlox (*Phlox subulata*) and basket-of-gold (*Aurinia saxatilis*) fill a slope in front of a sweep of daffodils.

▶ A walk down the residential section of Commercial Street in Providence is a gardener's delight. Flowers fill front yards and tumble over walls and arbors.

▶▶ Rows of hydrangeas, a bed bursting with red crocosmia, and inviting porch furniture make Bobby Kelley and Glenn Daidone's front garden the picture of summer pleasures. The garden, designed by Leo Manske, is a mix of summer-blooming shrubs and perennials.

really too small for a lawn, for example, or a steep slope that makes mowing difficult. People who are on the go have little time to relax in the backyard, so placing the garden by the front door makes sure that they see it every time they pull in and out of their driveway or walk into the house.

The flexible or inventive gardener takes advantage of the space available, and if this means putting the vegetable garden by the front door, or the wildflower meadow next to the street, then so be it. Cutting gardens can be grown in pots next to the garage, and a fruit tree trained as an es-

Some gardens are created as a gift for total strangers. This strip of land next to Main Street in Brewster isn't visible from the house, but a colorful tumble of yellow coreopsis *(Coreopsis grandiflora)*, blue cornflower or bachelor's buttons *(Centaurea cyanus)*, pink none-so-pretty or catchfly *(Silene armeria)*, and white yarrow *(Achillea millefolium)* was planted for all passersby to enjoy.

palier by the driveway. When it comes to lovely Cape landscapes, anything goes.

The home landscaper often realizes that the beautiful gardens that give a property curb appeal also contribute to the look of the entire neighborhood. When gardeners are in residence on any particular street, everyone benefits, and one front-yard garden will often inspire neighbors to expand or upgrade their plantings.

Whether a beautiful landscape is planted out of necessity, practicality, or the desire to improve the appearance of the house, a front-yard garden is ultimately a gift to everyone who goes by.

▲ David Kirchner and Scott Warner have placed their delightful cottage garden in the front of their property in Truro, where everyone who walks past it will be charmed.

▶ Wildflower seeds, an old stump, and a sense of humor were successfully combined to make an otherwise bare stretch of land next to Route 6A into a charming garden.

▲&▶ It's easy to see why Nancy Walsh has named her home "La Maison des Fleurs": her entire property is filled with flower gardens. The front yard contains several varieties of hydrangeas, oriental lilies, and assorted annuals, making this South Yarmouth garden a treat for all who drive by.

▶▶▲ Yellow hawkweed and wild daisies bloom with abandon in the field next to the Marstons Mills Airport. The Town of Barnstable owns and preserves this piece of property so that all may enjoy a small-town airfield and the timeless beauty of the open field filled with wildflowers.

▶▶ Colorful sap buckets await an inspired gardener's hand

▶▶▶ Perennial Stokes' asters (*Stokesia laevis*) and annual petunias make a colorful planting where a driveway meets the road.

## When a Passion for Plants Goes Public

When an individual's passion for plants is so great, it can grow into a treasure for everyone else. On Cape Cod there are several gardeners whose enthusiasm for gardens, and labors on the land, is generously shared with the public.

### The Rose Man

Life can take us down roads we never intended to travel, and for Dr. Irwin Ehrenreich, an unexpected and traumatic route led him into a Cape Cod rose garden.

Irwin grew up in Brooklyn, New York, and graduated

◄◄ All types of roses fill every corner of the Ehrenreichs' garden in Barnstable.

◄ Although it is doubtful that many roses grew around this house when it was built in the late 1600s, they now seem the perfect foundation planting for the renovated home, which is surrounded by a rose garden.

▲▲ The Rose Man's garden is a kaleidoscope of color in June, as climbers, shrub, and hybrid tea roses are at their peak of bloom.

▲ Irwin Ehrenreich, the Rose Man, has planted 'Bonica', one of Cape Cod's favorite shrub roses, along the stone wall that separates the rose garden from the driveway.

from Brooklyn College and New York University Medical School. He did his residency in otolaryngology (ear, nose, and throat), and it was at this time that he met his wife, Cindy. Irwin and Cindy lived in Connecticut for seven years while Irwin was in a private practice. In 1993 the couple,

# The Rose Man's Recommendations

Irwin Ehrenreich recommends these twelve easy-care, disease-resistant roses for Cape Cod gardens.

## Shrub roses

'Bonica'—pale pink blossoms cover this tall shrub in late June.

'Distant Drums'—peachy-pink flowers on a shrub around 4 feet tall.

'Knockout'—the original 'Knockout' rose has dark foliage and bright pink blooms all summer on 3- to 4-foot-tall shrubs.

"Meidiland Series"—several colors, including the ever-blooming 'Scarlet Meidiland'.

"Carefree Series"—several types of flowers and colors, including 'Carefree Beauty', which has large pink flowers and good repeat bloom.

## Grandiflora

'About Face'—a bicolor rose that ranges from bronzy-pink to pale peach.

## Floribunda

'Livin' Easy'—semi-double coral/apricot/yellow flowers on a plant that grows 4–5 feet high.

'Easy Going'—fragrant, golden yellow flowers on 4- to 5-foot plants.

## Climbers

'Climbing America'—bright coral flowers that have reliable repeat bloom when deadheaded all season.

'Autumn Sunset'—golden flowers are said to repeat bloom on this climbing rose.

'Iceberg'—heavy, clear white flowers in June, with sporadic repeat flowering the rest of the summer.

'New Dawn'—pale pink flowers cover this strong, fast-growing climber in June.

---

now with three young boys, moved to the Cape so that Irwin could join the staff of Hyannis Ear, Nose and Throat and the Cape Cod Hospital.

A run-down, three-hundred-year-old house caught their attention when they were hunting for a place to live. The house was built in 1690 and had been on the market for ten years when the Ehrenreichs noticed it. They remember that their realtor didn't even want to show it to them.

It was understandable that the broker didn't think that

◀◀ 'Royal Sunset' climbing roses are trained over the fence at the Rose Man Nursery in Barnstable. Although it's not visible in the photograph, a small sign on this fence dedicates the rose garden to Irwin's wife, Cindy.

◀◀ Part of the charm of this rose garden is the small details, such as the bench filled with pots and watering cans, that complement the roses. Here, yellow 'Graham Thomas' and a red shrub rose flower near the container display.

◀ Irwin pots up and grows hundreds of roses every year at the nursery on Route 6A. When you see the pots of flowering plants in June, it's hard to believe that they were small, bare-root plants just three months ago.

it was the proper home for a doctor and his family. The property had been neglected for years, and there were leaks in the roof, moldy carpeting over the wood floors, and a crumbling shingled exterior. Broken shutters bracketed the windows, and plaster was falling off the walls and ceilings. Many of the floors needed to be rebuilt because they sagged into the middle of the rooms. Outdoors, the property had also been ignored for years, and the overgrown landscaping was covered with brush and ivy.

None of this deterred Irwin and Cindy. Dr. Ehrenreich had worked on their house in Connecticut, and as an accomplished artist, Cindy was ready to paint walls and apply a faux marble finish to some of the floors. They recall that for some time they lived with plastic sheeting that separated the finished areas from those still being repaired.

Remodeling the house, and life as a physician, continued uneventfully until April 1996, when Irwin, working on a restoration project in his shop, severely injured his hand with a table saw. He was transferred from Cape Cod Hospital to Mass General, where doctors attempted to reattach two fingers. Only one of the fingers survived, and that one has just minimal use. Dr. Ehrenreich's career as a surgeon was suddenly over.

Three months after the accident, Irwin recalls that Cindy dragged him to a local rose show sponsored by the Seaside Rosarians. Roses have a way of working magic on many people, and Irwin was no exception. He remembers that he joined the Rosarians the same day and took home a free miniature rose. He needed something to take his mind off his misfortune, so shortly after that day, he bought a book about roses and decided to learn everything he could about this classic flower.

Irwin believes that being a surgeon requires a great deal of focus, dedication, and passion, and that the zeal he once had for surgery was transferred to his new interest in roses. He read everything he could about roses, made repeat visits to local nurseries, and began to design a rose garden for the front of his house.

Irwin built fences, trellises, and an arbor, where he mounted a sign that reads, "Rose garden by Irwin Ehrenreich—Inspired by Cindy Ehrenreich." Irwin explains that Cindy always wanted him to plant a rose garden because the flowers are beautiful and they have such a long and interesting history. He was also intrigued by the challenge of growing something that has a reputation for being difficult.

As time went on, Irwin's interest in roses expanded from hybrid teas to climbers, shrub roses, and miniatures. In addition, he began exploring the propagation and growth of old garden roses and species plants. In 2005 he opened his rose garden to the public and began propagating plants that he offers for sale.

A neighbor who has an old garden rose collection has sparked his curiosity about rambling roses, including some that were developed on Cape Cod. In the early 1900s M. H. Walsh bred rambling roses in Woods Hole, and Irwin hopes to bring them back into cultivation. He plans to propagate Walsh roses so that Cape Cod's own rose plants will once again be available to Cape gardeners.

## Coonamessett Farm

Although much of the Cape's farmland has been sold for development, there are pockets where commercial agriculture still flourishes and where garden lovers may still buy freshly cut garden flowers and just-harvested berries and vegetables. One such treasure is Coonamessett Farm on Hatchville Road in Falmouth.

Bordering Pickerel Pond, the rolling fields at Coonamessett are a mélange of hoop houses, pens of exotic and farm animals, a boat rental, a restaurant and general store, and fields of vegetables, small fruits, and flowers.

Local residents who have joined the membership program can pick their own produce, and everyone enjoys the

◄◄ The unassuming sign at the entrance to the farm doesn't hint at the abundance that awaits farther up the driveway. Just beyond the store, rows of blueberries, tomatoes, flowers, herbs, and vegetables fill the fields, assorted plants grow in the greenhouses, and a variety of animals roam the pens.

▲ Rows of vegetables and cutting flowers make the fields at Coonamessett Farm a colorful patchwork that covers the hills.

◄ Long rows of flowers, herbs, and vegetables are mulched with plastic, which keeps the sandy soil moist and helps prevent weeds.

farm atmosphere while picking up produce and gifts or garden items at the farm store. The café serves farm-grown produce at lunch, and at dinner on selected evenings, through the summer. Sitting on the store and restaurant's broad front porch, diners have a bucolic view of sloping fields filled with rows of colorful crops.

Ron and Roxanna Smolowitz have run the twenty-acre farm since 1984. Before buying the farm, Ron worked as a corps commander at the National Oceanic and Atmospheric Administration, and Roxanna is a veterinarian.

Although their mission statement says that the farm is "dedicated to the responsible stewardship and maintenance of the biodiversity of our planet," another of Ron's objectives seems to be to have fun. Association categories range from a twenty-dollar Elementary Family Membership to a thousand-dollar "Filthy Rich Donation"; the sign-up form states that membership benefits include the "right to pick crops inclusive of any attached insects" and the "right to paint 'Coonamessett Farm' on car or truck for tax purposes."

▲▲◀ Rows of purple coneflower (*Echinacea purpurea*), yarrow (*Achillea*), globe amaranth (*Gomphrena globosa*), and marigolds (*Tagetes*) do duel duty in a garden: they provide delightful summer bouquets and attract a range of beneficial insects to the garden.

▲▲ In the Coonamessett Farm clubhouse a blackboard announces which crops are ready for picking, and stacks of buckets wait for members to fill them with freshly harvested produce.

▲ A fleet of wagons waits for farm members who come to pick fresh berries, flowers, and vegetables.

# Growing Veggies on Cape Cod

Locate vegetable gardens in the sunniest area on your property. Most vegetables need at least five hours of sun, including the noon hour, when the sun is at its strongest.

Add compost or composted manure to the soil every fall or spring. Easily available soil amendments include composted leaves (don't worry, they do *not* make soil more acidic), seaweed (you don't have to rinse it), and dried or composted grass clippings. Such organic amendments can be spread on the surface of the garden anytime and turned into the soil in the spring.

Grow your own soil amendments. Sow winter rye in the garden in late September or early October, and turn the plants into the soil in early May.

Baby, it's cold outside! Those off-ocean winds are chilly, so don't plant heat-loving veggies too early. You can plant broccoli, cabbage, Brussels sprouts, peas, and lettuce in late April to early May, but wait to plant tomatoes, basil, peppers, beans, cucumbers, and squash until the end of May or early June.

Vegetables have a few short months to grow, so fertilize once a month with the fertilizer of your choice. Unless you are using an organic fertilizer such as fish and seaweed emulsion, always fertilize after the garden has been well watered. Never fertilize a thirsty plant! Fish and seaweed emulsion makes a good foliar feed for vegetables; mix it with water in a pressure sprayer, and apply it

to the foliage every two weeks.

Mulch your garden with straw, hay, bark mulch, chopped leaves, dried grass clippings, paper, or plastic. This will keep the ground moist and prevent weed seeds from germinating. Leave some space between the mulch and the stems of your plants, however, as piling mulch against the plants can keep the area too moist, which creates the perfect conditions for diseases to develop.

Water deeply, and water less often. It is better to water every four to six days, depending on the weather; keep your sprinkler or soaker hose on for at least two hours, so that plants will grow deep roots but the surface of the soil will have time to dry out between each watering.

Use a product containing Spinosad for control of caterpillars and most larvae of leaf-eating beetles. Spinosad is made of a naturally occurring bacteria, so you can spray it on edible crops. Do not spray Spinosad on flowering plants during the daytime, however, because it is not good for foraging bees.

Plants that like a long, hot growing season, such as peppers, eggplant, and melon, may not do well on Cape Cod. If you want to try growing heat-loving fruit and vegetables, try creating a tent-like greenhouse out of floating row cover. This sheer, lightweight fabric will help protect young plants from the early-summer cool temperatures and will accelerate their growth.

## The Lavender Farm

Local produce of a different kind is found growing at the end of long dirt drive in Harwich. Next to the parking lot is a small, wooden building that is ornamented with birdhouses and climbing roses, and if you've arrived in early July, the air is perfumed with lavender.

The Cape Cod Lavender Farm started with four hundred lavender plants and a personal vision. Twenty years ago, when Cynthia and Matthew Sutphin settled on fifteen acres in Harwich, Cynthia wanted to plant lavender, but her initial research wasn't encouraging. Many people told her that lavender wouldn't grow on Cape Cod because the climate and soil weren't quite right. But despite this early advice, Cynthia decided to try it anyway.

Though it is true that some varieties of lavender aren't suitable for this region, many species and cultivars do quite well, and the initial four hundred plants that the Sutphins put into the ground thrived.

◄◄ The Lavender Farm started with four hundred plants that grew in this area near Cynthia and Matthew Sutphin's house. Although the original plantings have been replaced and many larger fields have been planted, this area remains under cultivation with a type of lavender that blooms in July.

▲◄ Bags of harvested lavender sit in an old metal bin, perfuming the farm store before they are used to scent a car, closet, or drawer.

▲ The morning sun illuminates the first field where lavender was planted on the Sutphins' farm in Harwich.

The following spring Matthew bought Cynthia ten thousand lavender plants as a gift, and the Cape Cod Lavender Farm was well under way. The lavender flourished, and within a couple of years the Sutphins decided to open the farm to the public.

Although lavender is a very well-liked plant now, it wasn't as well known when Matthew and Cynthia started the farm. They recall that the earliest visitors were surprised that the fragrance they were loosely familiar with came

from a flower. Everyone left enchanted by the lavender plants, the layout of the farm, and the lavender products that Cynthia sold in the store.

Lavender blossoms are harvested in late June into July, and after cutting they are either bunched for sale or dried. After the harvest the plants are pruned to keep them round and bushy, and to stimulate some new summer growth. Cynthia believes that a second light pruning, done in the fall, is important for keeping the plants in good shape through the winter.

The Sutphins report that the two biggest challenges are the weeds in the summertime and the weather in the late winter and early spring. Weeding is an ongoing chore, although Cynthia says that it is satisfying to see it done. There is not much that can be done about the Cape's typically cold spring weather, however, and this season can be

harder on the lavender plants than the harsh conditions of winter. After the coldest months are over, the Sutphins hold their breaths until the weather warms.

Over the years Matthew and Cynthia have not only added to and cared for the lavender fields, but expanded the gardens to create woodland walking trails and other plantings on the farm. The Enchanted Garden provides a shady area where visitors can retreat from the summer sun, and children enjoy the small stone castle that houses forest fairies.

Whether the lavender is in bloom or not, these green, idyllic acres and the enticing shop are clearly popular with residents and visitors alike. Matthew Sutphin says that people at the Harwich Chamber of Commerce have told him

▲◀ Several types of lavender fill the field in front of the Cape Cod Lavender Farm's store. When the field is in full bloom, visitors can smell the fragrance as soon as they park their cars.

▲ The shop at the Cape Cod Lavender Farm offers lavender plants, lavender products made by several local artisans, and a comfortable place to sit next to fields of flowers.

▶ Located down a long dirt road and surrounded by oak trees and swamp maples, the lavender farm is a magical place, apart from the bustle of everyday life. The colors, scent, setting, and overall aesthetic are captivating and soothing; any garden lover will fall in love with this pastoral spot.

◀ Cut stems of lavender are placed in plastic trays as they are harvested. After the harvest, Cynthia trims the shrubs so that they stay rounded and full. This pruning can stimulate a bit of new growth, and it helps prevent the plants from splitting open under the weight of a heavy snowfall.

# Tips for Growing Lavender

Lavender prefers a neutral to alkaline soil—find out what the pH of your soil is by having it tested at the Barnstable Cooperative Extension in Barnstable and, if needed, add lime or wood ashes to raise the pH.

Grow lavender in full sun—for healthy, flower-filled lavender you need at least a five-hour period of direct sun that includes the noon hour, and all-day sun is even better.

Keep lavender bushy and tight by pruning off deadwood in the spring and shearing off an inch or two of foliage after bloom and again in the fall. Never prune a lavender plant to the ground be-cause a drastic pruning of an older plant is likely to kill it. Overgrown, woody, sprawling shrubs should be replaced with new plants that are sheared annually to keep them tight and full.

Good drainage is a must for laven-der—if you have sandy soil, amend it before planting with compost or manure, but no peat moss.

Lavender likes heat, so it will thrive when mulched with white sand or mar-ble chips. If this small shrub is planted in a garden that is covered with bark mulch, keep the mulch away from the lavender stems to prevent the area from staying too moist.

Like most herbs, lavender should not be given much fertilizer. A light applica-tion of organic fertilizer in the early spring can be given if needed.

Too much water is the kiss of death for lavender: in a drought, water deeply once a week, but do not water frequent-ly, either by hand or with an automatic sprinkler system.

Harvest lavender in the morning when the flowers have just opened. Dry-ing it quickly in a dark, low-moisture place is the best way to preserve color and fragrance.

A castle for fairies is the focal point in the Lavender Farm's enchanted gar-den. Located in the shade to the side of the largest lavender field, this woodland garden is worth a visit even if the lavender isn't in bloom.

The dark purple flowers of 'Hidcote' lavender are always a favorite with Cape Cod gardeners and visitors to the Lavender Farm. This field will soon be harvested and the cut lavender will be bundled for sale or dried for use in sachets and other fragrant products.

that the question that they hear most frequently is "How do I get to Route 6?" but the *second* most popular query is "How do I get to the lavender farm?"

## A Masterful Garden

For some people, summer is not complete unless they make a trip to the Barnstable County Fair. Although they enjoy the rides, the concerts, and the normally forbidden fried foods, many admit that the animals and gardens are the attractions that bring them back every July.

Harry Bowen, a volunteer Master Gardener who has been instrumental in the gardens' care as well as their design, planned the fairground demonstration gardens in 1983. Once a week a group of Cape Cod Master Gardeners, under the direction of Roberta Clark, the Barnstable Cooperative Extension educator, tends to the gardens so that they are at their best during fair week.

The demonstration gardens are divided into several sections that contain perennials, vegetables, and herbs. Near the sidewalk that leads to food concessions and rides, the

It was in this herb garden that I learned a valuable lesson about spring cleanup and the resilience of plants. During my first year as a Master Gardener, I was helping clear out the gardens in April. I timidly clipped an inch or two off the winter-worn thyme, but after some minutes of trimming, the plants weren't much improved; I was nervous about cutting too much. As I puttered indecisively, Mary Lopez, an experienced Master Gardener, sat down beside me, gathered some thyme into one hand and quickly snipped it off right at ground level. Seeing my shock, Mary smiled at me. "Don't worry," she said, "it'll come back." It did, and it still does.

The path into the raised vegetable beds runs between the herbs and the butterfly garden, and it ends at the tent where the Master Gardeners offer garden advice and information. Next to the tent is an enclosed pen that protects the blueberries from birds and other critters.

perennial border showcases plants that bloom in July, with an emphasis on unusual or recently introduced varieties. Walking away from the perennial bed, fair visitors can visit the main garden by passing under a large arbor where trumpet vines are usually in full bloom at fair time.

Circling the large, fenced vegetable beds are a variety of gardens, the first of which consists of blueberry bushes that are caged to protect the berries from birds, chipmunks, and hungry fairgoers. Next to the blueberry pen is a gooseberry and raspberry bed, a wild, self-seeding butterfly garden, and

the more formally laid-out herb garden. Finally, there is an area where Roberta Clark or the Master Gardeners plant a different theme garden every summer.

It's the raised-bed vegetable gardens that draw the most attention, however. Filled with organically rich loam and amended every spring with composted cow manure, these gardens are always filled with impressive produce at fair time.

The cranelike flower buds on the fall-planted garlic and the artichokes always prompt comments or questions, and

▲ Beyond the butterfly garden the sturdy wooden tomato cages support several varieties of tomatoes, even though they often grow more than six feet tall.

▲▶ Pink balloon flower, purple coneflower, and 'Early Sunrise' coreopsis mingle with pale yellow pincushion flower *(Scabiosa ochroleuca)* in the Cooperative Extension's butterfly garden.

▶ The Cape Organic Gardeners created this display in the horticulture tent at the fair. The tent also contains a display of prize flowers and foliage and spectacular flower arrangements created by members of local garden clubs.

many admire the sturdy and attractive wooden tomato supports. Several varieties of lettuce grow along with squash, chard, onions, potatoes, beans, cabbage, and the other vegetables that fill the beds. All are irrigated with soaker hoses that are on a timer, and problems are dealt with using the least toxic pest and disease controls.

At the far end of the garden is a bed that is higher than all the others; it was designed to be handicapped-accessible, and every year it is planted and maintained by Inez Narbis, a Master Gardener who is in a wheelchair. Inez shows fair visitors that just about everyone can grow plants and get pleasure from gardening.

▲▲ The landscape reawakens at the Olde Cottage Garden, designed by Jeffrey Thomas. A reed fence separates this display garden from the surrounding tangle of brush and vines, and natural wood plant supports are both functional and ornamental.

▲▶ A shingled garden shed, a door and box painted blue, and some charming twig supports turn a utilitarian building into a romantic section of the garden. These are the start of a cottage garden created by Jeffrey Thomas.

▲ Jeffrey Thomas, a garden designer, created this seasonal display to celebrate autumnal gardens. The fading annuals were purposefully left as a base for the pumpkins, cornstalks, mums, cabbages, and kales because they soften the wall and underscore the conclusion of the growing season.

## Well Designed

A designer works with color, texture, and shape and, whether working indoors or out, is creating a visual experience and an ambiance. Jeffrey Thomas is a garden stylist with a singular flair and sensibility, and his work has been frequently seen at regional businesses, along Cape roadways, and on private properties.

Jeffrey is a designer of cottage gardens, but he also creates elaborate floral arrangements, outdoor displays, and vignettes for his customers in all seasons. Whether he is designing a composition for the spring cottage garden, producing a display that celebrates the harvest, or filling an urn with Christmas greens, Jeffrey creates a presentation that is rich with plants, props, and atmosphere.

▲◄ Even the utility area of the Olde Cottage Garden is attractive when pots and tools are piled into a wooden garden cart.

▲ As the roses fade the penstemon continues to bloom in the back of the garden. This garden remains attractive all summer because Jeffrey's design combines orderly lines of plants with clusters of shrubs and perennials. Adding to its all-season interest are strategically placed plants with foliage that isn't green.

◄ The back door is made beautiful with the use of Coco Plum's antiques. Jeffrey Thomas worked with a combination of garden furniture, antique tools, seasonal plants, and produce to commemorate the harvest and to dress up an otherwise bare area.

In the Town of Barnstable community gardens, several plots are joined together for use as a children's garden. Volunteer Master Gardeners assist many children in growing herbs, vegetables, and flowers. Because the children choose what they would like to grow, the garden is different every year. This season the garden contained a pole-bean teepee, a central path lined with marigolds, and a display of unique and charming scarecrows created by the children and the Master Gardeners.

## Rent to Grow

From one end of Cape Cod to the other, there are community gardens where those who want to grow vegetables and flowers are able to plant in good company. There are community gardens in Sandwich, Marstons Mills, Harwich, and Orleans, to name just a few. In such places, those who don't have enough space or enough sun to grow vegetables or herbs are able to rent a plot and grow what they like.

Some neighborhood gardens are on private land and others are on property owned by the town. Most provide a water system, and part of the rent goes to support the maintenance of the irrigation. A number of community gardens plow the land for the gardeners, though others do not till the soil, or they leave portions of it so that some renters can plant perennials or berry bushes that can develop from year to year.

Gardeners who rent a plot in community gardens gain the produce that is grown, but they also benefit from seeing how other people garden. Some choose to stake their tomatoes with old ski poles; others use bamboo or wire cages. One gardener uses paper mulch, but another chooses hay or plastic. Some keep their plot free of weeds, while others let the weeds grow. The wide variety of cultivation methods proves that there is no single right way to garden.

Whether the garden is grown to add curb appeal, for public education, because of a fascination with a particular plant, or as a means to produce a tasty tomato, Cape gardeners discover that the rewards of the garden are many and varied. And one of the most satisfying benefits for many gardeners is sharing their passion with others.

# Chapter 3

# OVER THE GARDEN GATE

## For Every House a Garden

Whether a property is several acres or several feet across, Cape Cod gardeners use the available space to cultivate beautiful gardens. And whether the owner is a confirmed do-it-yourself gardener or has the help of landscape professionals, it is possible for every Cape home to have a garden regardless of the size of the property or the style of the house.

In fact, the design of a building often dictates the type of garden planted. A classic shingled Cape Cod house practically calls for a cottage-style garden or a row of roses draped over a fence. Large contemporary Cape houses look appealing with a landscape that is slightly more manicured or formal than a cottage garden, but one that contains roses, inkberry holly, ornamental grasses, and other plants that are associated with the region.

Many colonial houses look best with a formal layout that uses larger plants to soften the tall, boxy exterior, or a fenced front-entry garden. And no matter what the house style, there is something very pleasing about bright blue hydrangeas next to gray shingles and freshly painted white trim.

These generalities aside, first and foremost a garden needs to please the homeowner. Your landscape should make you smile every time you look out the window or pull into your driveway, and if this means going against all design conventions, then so be it.

Gardens also need to work with their surroundings and the natural topography of the land. Large, open, flat areas often become more interesting when divided into outdoor rooms through the use of hedges, mixed shrub borders, fences and archways, or groupings of trees. This division of an open area is especially effective if there are openings in

the plantings that allow for a glimpse of the area beyond. Even loosely partitioned properties make the landscape more intimate, but the view from one area to the other also maintains a spacious feeling.

Although the Cape isn't known for its hills and valleys, there are areas where glacier-dumped rocks or man-made disturbances have created sloping landscapes. Many gardeners choose terracing as the best option for dealing with a slope that is more than thirty-five degrees. Such inclines are difficult to mow, and hard rain will quickly carry topsoil and mulch away. Timbers or stone walls create level planting areas that will prevent soil and valuable soil amendments from washing downhill.

In addition to making a steep grade plantable, terracing

▲◄ Some Cape gardeners choose formal foundation plantings, some rose gardens, and some perennial beds. But for many years Pam Eichin turned her talents and labor to raising cut flowers, herbs, and vegetables in Osterville. Pam, who is a professional gardener, planted all the annuals from seed, packing the zinnias in tightly so that the plants supported each other and crowded out weeds.

◄ Susan Makowski's house encloses this patio on three sides, creating three flower beds that surround a large brick patio. Susan uses this area to plant herbs and perennials, and she fills several containers with flowering annuals to create a display of flowers all summer. Cottage-style gardens frame the walkway to the patio, providing a relaxed, abundantly colorful mix of perennials and self-seeding annuals.

▲ Barbara Brown's barn was newly constructed to look old, and the mix of annuals and perennials in the surrounding flowerbeds creates an old-fashioned garden that looks as if it's been there for generations.

▲ As a professional landscape designer, the owner of this large property in Orleans made good use of a standard principle of garden design: dividing a large open space makes the landscape more interesting and intimate. Connie LeClair planned her garden to include several distinct areas containing plants that provide color and texture in all seasons. In September the airy texture of fountain grass (*Pennisetum alopecuroides* 'Hameln') is the perfect companion to the solidity and color of *Sedum* 'Autumn Joy'. The fence makes an ideal backdrop for the perennial border, and it screens the vegetable garden and utilitarian areas of the property.

can create beds that are more easily maintained. When you stand in a lower bed, it's possible to reach well into the one above without bending over. Terracing also creates a garden where all plants are well displayed, even if the specimen or clump in the rear is shorter than what is growing in the lower terrace.

Although terraces offer these benefits, they present some challenges as well. Soil amendments, plants, and tools must be hauled up to higher levels, and the strong structure of the terracing materials can dominate the look unless plants

▲ Ann Bennett always claimed that her love of gardening was in her genes. That may be so, but she had a singular touch with her plantings, and she generously worked to create gardens elsewhere in her community. She filled this combined shrub and perennial bed with many varieties of plants, including 'Bonica' roses, yellow coreopsis, salvia, perennial geraniums, and lavender.

▲▶ Arthur Clark has turned a standard, suburban-size property in Osterville into a lush oasis. Even the patio area, where the brickwork runs right up to the house, becomes a colorful garden with annuals in containers and hanging baskets that have been hung from the roof's edge at varying levels.

▲▶▶ Matt Mirisola and Ric Ide have focused their artistic talents on their backyard in Provincetown, turning a very steep slope that was once filled with brush and weeds into a dramatic garden. Using a combination of shrubs, trees, perennials, and annuals that are interspersed among stone walls, steps, and paths, they have created a landscape that is always color-

ful and ever-changing. Their use of short, horizontal rows of plants makes this narrow space look wider, and the addition of trees and sculptures adds vertical elements that break up the horizontal lines.

▶ In addition to color, movement is an important part of the Ide-Mirisola garden. Water splashes down a small waterfall, and butterflies and birds flit in and out as they visit whatever is blooming on the hillside. At the bottom of the hill are two Adirondack chairs, where Ric and Matt say they enjoy sitting to watch the constantly changing flow of life on the hillside. Ric Ide created the collection of ceramic finials that add another vertical focal point above the plants.

▶▶ What does an out-of-control plant person do on a very small property? She or he gardens in every available spot, including containers on benches and terraced slopes. Here assorted annuals fill the pots in an ever-changing display of color, and bright gold Stella d'Oro daylilies bloom in the beds. The terraces are particularly prized because they ring the deck, making it a very private space.

The author's terraced garden bursts into color in late April as the creeping phlox and azaleas come into bloom, and the yellow Hakone grass emerges next to the purple foliage of Weigela 'Midnight Wine'.

are used to moderate their prominence. It's advisable when planting on terraced beds to use some vertical plants or ornaments to break up the hard horizontal lines that the timbers or rocks create. Plants that drape over the wall also can soften these structures.

Whether gardens are placed next to the house, in terraces, or elsewhere on a property, the choice of plants used in Cape Cod gardens goes well beyond flowering shrubs, perennials, and mown grass. Some Cape homeowners choose to landscape their property in less traditional ways. Large cutting gardens filled with zinnias or dahlias are popular with some; others choose to use edible plants that provide for their table and their landscaping.

In June the author's backyard terraces are filled with biennial foxglove (*Digitalis purpurea*) and feverfew (*Chrysanthemum parthenium*). The potted annuals make a changeable display.

▲ Barbara Stewart rejected traditional foundation evergreens in favor of flowering perennials that provide a succession of blooms from spring through fall. The scalloped edging and the low fence emphasize the cottage quality of this doorstep garden.

◄ On a September morning sunlight streams through the woods surrounding the Kruegers' house in Truro. With apple trees in the background, the sun lights the asparagus foliage behind Nancy Krueger's pink fall anemones.

Every gardener knows that gardens change from year to year and evolve over the decades. Some of these alterations are deliberate and some just seem to progress on their own. Susan Ambrose once had a vegetable garden in this rustically fenced area, but over time the area turned into a wildflower garden.

Raised beds are an especially popular way to neatly contain herbs, vegetables, and flowers for cutting. Constructing low walls of timber or stone also allows the soil to be more easily amended; loam and composted manure can be dug into the native soil, and then more amended loam is used to fill the enclosure, the result being a deeply improved planting bed. The paths in between raised beds are either planted with grass, paved with bricks, or covered with stones, crushed clamshells, or bark mulch.

Edible landscaping needn't be confined to specific areas.

◀▲ For some gardens there is one season when they are in their glory, but Bill and Carolyn Ray's garden is captivating throughout the year. In spring, tulips and other bulbs complement the cottage-style house, and the boxwoods that line the walkway echo the shape of the dwarf Alberta spruce on either side of the front door. From midsummer until fall, purple coneflower, black-eyed Susans, and 'Autumn Joy' sedum fill the front beds, and the peegee hydrangea tree (*Hydrangea paniculata* 'Grandiflora') is loaded with pinkish-white flowers.

▲▲ The placement of a few plants can define an entire garden, and the structure of these espaliered apple trees adds charm to this yard even when they aren't in bloom. The fence and espaliers polish the end of the Rays' driveway and create a back garden that is screened from the street.

▲ Polly and Mel Coté say that their courtyard garden requires plenty of work but no mowing! They have filled the yard with raised vegetable beds separated by crushed-clamshell paths. Other landscaping is also done with edible plants: a grapevine drapes itself over the fence, espaliered apple trees fill one wall, and blueberry bushes are planted in a sunny corner.

Shrubs and trees that produce fruit are popular garden plants, and vegetables combine well in pots and borders. Blueberries, for example, make attractive foundation plantings; they provide sweet flowers in the springtime, fruit in July, and brilliantly colored foliage in the fall. Herbs such as parsley and basil and seeded leaf lettuce can be combined with flowering annuals in containers and window boxes, and red-stemmed chard fits nicely in perennial beds. Adding such edibles to standard landscaping is especially smart on properties where space is limited.

# Low-Maintenance Perennials for Cape Cod

Perennial plants are considered to be low maintenance when they return reliably for at least three years, need only a weekly soaking during a drought, don't need frequent division, editing, or staking, and are basically carefree except for deadheading after they flower.

False indigo (*Baptisia australis*) is most commonly referred to by its genus name, *Baptisia*. This is a must-have plant in the Cape Cod garden because it is easy and attractive all summer. Baptisia is a long-lived, drought-tolerant perennial that blooms in June and has attractive blue-gray foliage the rest of the season. *Baptisia australis* has dark blue flowers, but varieties with yellow, purple, and bicolor blooms are also available. False indigo grows to about 4 feet tall and 3 feet wide, depending on the variety. Because this plant is often small when purchased, and the plants don't transplant well, care should be taken when planting to provide sufficient room for this perennial to grow. The only maintenance this plant needs is the removal of the large and somewhat clunky seedpods after bloom. *Baptisia* grows best in full sun and well-drained soil.

Balloon flower (*Platycodon grandiflo-rum*) blooms in July with round, balloon-like buds that open to star-shaped flowers. Available with blue, white, or pink flowers, balloon flower has a taproot, so it is drought-tolerant but does not transplant well. Tall varieties can be floppy, but there are several dwarf forms that stay under 12 inches tall. Balloon flower thrives in organically amended sandy soils, and it prefers five or more hours of direct sun.

Phlox 'David' (*Phlox paniculata* 'David') is a disease-resistant variety of summer phlox, a perennial plant that is well known for its susceptibility to powdery mildew. 'David' is usually disease-free, however, and the 4- to 5-foot-tall plants are topped with huge white flowers in July and August. A good cut flower and back-of-the-border perennial, phlox 'David' is also fragrant on hot summer evenings. Plant this phlox in full sun and divide it every seven to ten years if the clump becomes too large.

Stokes' aster (*Stokesia laevis*) blooms in midsummer and never needs dividing. Available with blue, purple, yellow, white, or pink flowers, Stokes' asters grow in full sun and are beautiful when planted in front of daylilies. Some vari-eties stay under 12 inches tall and others grow over 2 feet high. The only mainte-nance that Stokes' asters need is cutting flower stems back to the foliage after flowering has finished.

Moonbeam coreopsis (*Coreopsis verti-cillata* 'Moonbeam') has light, ferny foliage and hundreds of pale yellow flowers that bloom from late June until well into August or even September. 'Moonbeam' is drought-tolerant and does not spread as quickly as other varieties of threadleaf coreopsis. Like all coreopsis, it prefers a garden that receives at least five hours of sun. The only negative thing you could say about this plant is that it can be short-lived and may need replacing every three to five years.

Hardy hibiscus (*Hibiscus moscheutos*) plants are available in short, medium, and tall varieties, and the huge, showy flowers are spectacular in late July, August, or September, depending on the variety. All the gardener has to provide is full sun, amended soil, and enough room to grow. The round flowers come in a range of colors including white, pink, red, and yellow. Some varieties have red throats and white or pink outer petals.

This perennial returns reliably but it is very late to break dormancy and often doesn't emerge from the soil until June.

Russian sage (*Perovskia atriplicifolia*) produces a cloud of lavender flowers from early July until frost. Although Russian sage grows 3 to 4 feet tall, the flower spires are wispy so it often looks good when placed in groups of three or five plants. *Perovskia* is drought-tolerant and is especially attractive when planted near ornamental grasses in full sun. Unlike most perennials that do better when given minimal amounts of fertilizer, Russian sage benefits from a midsummer application of liquid fertilizer.

Coneflower (*Echinacea purpurea*) is the perfect plant for cutting gardens and perennial borders and for mixing with flowering shrubs. Once called purple coneflower because most varieties were a shade of purple-pink, echinacea is now available in white, yellow, mango, orange, and dark pink, and new colors and cultivars are being introduced every year. Coneflowers are most attractive when planted close together in groups of five or more, and their central cones are pretty in the garden long after the petals have wilted away. Grow echinacea in well-drained soil and full or part sun.

Daylilies (*Hemerocallis* species and hybrids) are available in many colors and sizes, from the old-fashioned orange "ditch lilies" to the clump-growing hybrids that are available in hundreds of colors, shapes, and sizes. Short, early-blooming varieties such as 'Stella d'Oro' and 'Happy Returns' will rebloom in late summer if promptly deadheaded after the first flowering. Other cultivars bloom in July or August, and some, such as 'Final Touch', are still producing flowers into September. Daylilies thrive in full or part sun, and they are drought-tolerant. Like Russian sage, which combines well with daylilies, *Hemerocallis* hybrids appreciate a midsummer application of liquid fertilizer. The appearance of daylilies is improved by promptly removing the bare stems that remain after flowering finishes.

Liatris (*Liatris* species and cultivars) are occasionally called blazing stars or gay feather, but they are most commonly referred to as *Liatris*. This midsummer perennial is native to North America and has the unusual characteristic of blooming from the top down. Available in shades of lavender or white, *Liatris* is drought-tolerant but prefers organically amended and well-drained soil. *Liatris* works well in a mixed perennial border and in butterfly gardens, and it should be planted in full or part sun.

Giant fleece flower (*Persicaria polymorpha*) is an underused perennial that deserves a place in more gardens. Growing 5 to 6 feet high, this *Persicaria* looks like an astilbe on steroids. Fleece flower is more drought-tolerant than astilbe, however, and the white flowers are in bloom for a much longer period. *Persicaria polymorpha* requires organically rich soil, and it grows well in full sun to part shade. There are many worthy plants in the genus *Persicaria*, including the long-flowering cultivar 'Firetail', but there are others, such as 'Painter's Palette', that self-seed so prolifically that they should be sold with a disclaimer. Fleece flowers are a good example of the wisdom of knowing the complete botanic name and researching a plant's characteristics before placing it in the garden.

Hosta (*Hosta* species and cultivars) is one of the most cast-iron plants you can place in the landscape. There are hostas that are low groundcovers and those that grow to be huge specimen plants. Hostas are available with a wide range of leaf shapes and colors as well, and the plant is usually more sun-tolerant than most people realize. In all but the hottest sun or in part or full shade, hosta is a wonderful component in foundation plantings or perennial beds.

Foamflower (*Tiarella cordifolia*) is the perfect companion plant for hostas. This long-flowering perennial is drought-tolerant, and there are many cultivars that have attractive dark-splotched foliage as well as pinkish-white bottlebrush flowers. Foamflower thrives in part sun or part shade, grows to about 12 inches high, and blooms from May into July when deadheaded as blooms go by.

*Epimedium* (*Epimedium* species) is one of the best groundcovers for dry shade. Once established, *Epimedium*'s heart-shaped leaves grow so thickly that weeds don't stand a chance. The only maintenance this plant requires is a late-winter shearing to the ground to remove the cold-damaged foliage. *Epimedium*'s delicate flowers appear in April, but it is the foliage that makes this a desirable perennial. This plant thrives in enriched garden soil in full or part shade, and most varieties grow 8 to 12 inches high.

## Sun and Shade

The topography and size of a property are two factors that determine the look of a Cape Cod garden, but another influence is the amount of sun or shade that the site receives. Because different plants grow best with varying amounts of sunlight, this is the most important feature that influences the look and style of a Cape garden. For many on the Cape, the challenge isn't in where to plant, but in determining if their property is in full sun, part sun, part shade, or full shade.

For gardeners, full sun is defined as six hours or more of dead-on sunshine, including the period from 11:00 AM to 2:00 PM. The hours just before and after the noon hour are when the sun is strongest, so plants that thrive in full sun need to have unrestricted sunlight during that period. Plants that will thrive in part sun need at least four hours of sunlight, also including the noon hour.

Part shade is also defined as at least four hours of sun, but those hours could be in the early morning, late afternoon, or a combination of the two. If a garden receives no direct sun at all, the area is said to be in full shade, and gardens that get some filtered sun through the canopy of trees are also considered to be full shade landscapes.

When most people imagine a garden for their Cape Cod property, they picture roses, hydrangeas, and large groups of assorted flowering perennials, and if their proper-

◄◄ Under the shade of oak trees, Dave and Judy Rogers have created a cooling place for people *and* cats. A glance at the Rogerses' garden makes it clear why Dave's design business is called Art in Green.

▲◄ One of the sunniest areas on the Schoonover property is near the back deck, so a mixed annual and perennial garden is planted where it's visible from the porch and the house. Even in this flowerbed, however, amounts of sunlight vary greatly from one end of the border to the other, so those plants that prefer full sun are grouped on the left, while shade-tolerant annuals and perennials fill the other end of the garden.

◄ A garden shed not only is functional in a shade garden, but provides solidity and structure that contrast well with the assortment of green foliage. This relatively new shade garden is jointly designed and maintained by Will Clarke, of Perennial Solutions, and the homeowner, Helen Schoonover. The mound of *Geranium macrorrhizum*, one of the best plants for dry shade, grows in front of a selection of hostas, ferns, and hydrangeas.

▲ Yellow varieties of *Hakonechloa macra* grass are the perfect companion for hostas in a shade garden, and objects such as the vase in the Schoonover garden can add color to an area that contains a large amount of green.

ty is in full or part sun, their vision can become a reality. Even plants such as impatiens and hosta, commonly thought to do best in shade, will thrive in sunny gardens provided the soil is well amended and regularly watered. But plants that prefer sun usually cannot be grown in shade; when plants don't receive the necessary amount of sunlight, they grow leggy and fail to bloom.

Some Cape gardeners thin out stands of trees, taking out pitch pines, for example, and leaving only the oaks. Others remove several lower limbs or eliminate branches so that although the property is still shaded, the cover is less dense and filtered sunlight is allowed to come through. Removing all the trees in selected areas is an option that cre-

ates some sunny sections while retaining the nicest mature trees and the cooling shade that they create.

Whether the sunlight arrives through oak trees or around the corner at the end of the day, shade is shade, but fortunately there are several plants that will thrive in little to no direct sunlight. Many of the plants that do well in shady areas are prized not for their flowers but for the color and texture of their foliage. Hostas are a particular favorite for shade because they are available in all sizes and often have yellow or white variegation or bluish leaves. These

▲▲ John Figmic planted this lush shade garden in Osterville. Variegated Solomon's seal *(Polygonatum odoratum)*, *Epimedium*, and ostrich fern *(Matteuccia struthiopteris)* add varying shades of green, and these cooling hues are echoed by the choice of furniture color.

▲ This Marstons Mills shade garden is planted with rhododendrons and Exbury azaleas for early spring color, hosta and *Heuchera* for foliage color, and astilbe for summer blooms.

perennials are also adaptable and easy to grow, and variegated varieties brighten shady gardens even on foggy days.

Ferns are good companions for hostas because the fine texture of a fern's foliage contrasts with the solid form of the hosta. Lady fern *(Athyrium filix-femina)* is especially nice for Cape gardens because it grows into a large, gracefully shaped clump, but it doesn't spread or take over the garden.

Japanese painted ferns *(Athyrium nipponicum* 'Pictum') is in the same genus as the lady fern, but it is shorter and spreads its fronds somewhat horizontally, and its foliage is often tinted with silver and purple.

Most grasses don't do well in the shade, but when a garden receives at least two hours of sun, hakone grass *(Hakonechloa macra)* adds a soft, drapey texture to the garden, and the varieties 'Aureola' and 'All Gold' are a colorful bright yellow. It is the texture and color of this grass that is so attractive in combination with other shade-loving plants.

Gardeners with shady properties don't have to be content with colored foliage, however. There are several plants that provide a show of flowers in the shade, especially when massed. The native foamflower *(Tiarella cordifolia)* is covered

with white bottlebrush flowers that are tinged with pink. This tidy, low perennial blooms from early May well into July, and many cultivars have dark, blotched foliage that continues to be interesting after the flowers fade.

Rocket *Ligularia* (*Ligularia stenocephala* 'The Rocket') requires well-amended and well-watered soil, but it's worth the extra attention for the show of yellow spires that appear in July. This perennial makes the perfect companion to blue hydrangeas and white impatiens, and even after the blooms fade, the large, jagged-edged leaves are assets in a shady flowerbed.

A few shrubs that do well in shady Cape gardens include rhododendrons, summersweet (*Clethra alnifolia*), and oakleaf hydrangeas (*Hydrangea quercifolia*). Summersweet

▲◀ When the author moved into this house, she wanted a flower garden to be the first "room" anyone entered. Because this area was also the sunniest part of the property, it was the perfect place for cottage-style perennials such as foxglove.

▲ Foxglove (*Digitalis purpurea*) is a biennial, which means that it grows foliage the first year, blooms the next year, and then dies. Like most biennials, however, foxglove self-seeds where the growing conditions are favorable. The amount of spring rain or winter snow can influence how many seeds germinate and the number of seedlings that survive the winter. The bumper crop shown here is a gift from the snowy winter of 2005.

and oakleaf hydrangeas are both adaptable native plants that are valued for summer flowering and attractive fall foliage color, and the many varieties of rhododendrons are Cape Cod's favorite evergreen shrubs.

In this sunny cottage garden a mix of Shasta daisies, purple coneflower, *Liatris*, lady bells, and yellow *Anthemis* daisies mingle with annual *Cleome* in front of the sparkling foliage of inkberry holly. Well placed in front of a butter-colored house with purple shutters, Sivert Johnston's cottage garden completes the perfect picture of summer on the Cape.

Gardeners who have areas of shade *and* sun are especially blessed, for they have access to the full range of foliage and flowering plants. From roses and Russian sage to hydrangeas with eye-catching blue blooms, part- and full-sun gardens can have it all. But amounts of sunlight vary with the seasons and with the growth of surrounding plants, so as Cape gardeners put plants in place, they must be aware of adjacent vegetation.

That line of shrubs that looks so good behind a newly planted perennial garden, the small tree that is ringed with flowering annuals, and the neighbor's Leyland cypress screen will all grow larger, allowing less and less sunlight in to neighboring plants. Fortunately, gardeners tend to be a flexible bunch, and sun-loving plants can usually be moved to a brighter location as neighboring plants grow.

John Sullivan's front garden is shady in the morning and sunny in the afternoon, when the sun is the strongest. Most sun-loving plants, like the black-eyed Susan (*Rudbeckia* 'Goldsturm'), purple coneflower (*Echinacea purpurea*), and summer phlox (*Phlox paniculata*), will do well with a half day of sunshine.

## Passageways

Steps and walkways don't have to be mere paths to get from one place to another. Cape Cod gardeners use these spaces to create gardens that are attractive and functional. Whether the corridor is made of stepping-stones, pavers, or gravel, small plants can grow in the path itself, and no matter what materials are used, flowerbeds can be placed on either side of the passageway.

A frequently used path, the entry into a house, or the walkway between the house and the garage are places of maximum exposure and so are the perfect place to site a garden. Areas that get less foot traffic but are difficult to mow, or too shady for a lawn, also make good corridor gardens, especially when the right plants are selected.

Because most pathway materials hold heat, plants that are placed around pavers and stones in full sun need to be heat- and drought-tolerant. Thyme, chamomile, and low-growing sedums are good choices to position in the path itself, and dianthus, lavender, low varieties of catmint or

▲◄ Lady's mantle (*Alchemilla mollis*) and poppies spill from this richly planted garden into the arch-covered path.

▲ Heath, heather, and creeping thyme predominate in this stone-step garden planted by Virginia Dennis.

▲▶ A walkway to the main entrance doesn't have to be a straight passageway just for moving from here to there. The cobblestone path that leads to Dave and Judy Rogers's front door curves out into a small sitting area surrounded by a garden.

asters, and annual creeping verbena will thrive even when planted right next to that walk.

Part-shade paths have the perfect conditions for growing Labrador violets or Kenilworth ivy in cracks and crevices, and *Epimedium*, *Geranium macrorrhizum*, and low varieties of hosta are attractive and weed-smothering plants to grow next to walkways.

Many Cape shade gardens have paths and gardens where moss flourishes between stepping-stones or on the

▲ Rocks absorb and retain a great deal of the sun's heat, so a rock walkway is the perfect place to plant alpines, thyme, and other drought-tolerant plants.

▲◄ Turning left in the middle of this brick walk will bring you to the front door, and the path exits out both sides of the perennial garden, allowing sensible access to both sides of the yard and driveway.

◄◄ Assorted varieties of *Miscanthus* grass and the fall blooming sedum 'Autumn Joy' flank a thyme-and-flagstone path in a West Falmouth garden.

◄ Ann Bennett proved that sometimes even a patio or walkway can be a garden. Spaces left between rocks provide places for an assortment of shrubs and perennials to grow.

▲▲ Elizabeth Wolff carried wave-worn rocks up from the beach to make the path that leads to her front door. Assorted perennials, including veronica and dianthus, line the walk and fill the air with a sweet and spicy scent of cloves.

▲ A grass path is lined with Pennsylvania stone that has been sunk so that the top of the stone is at ground level. The stones form a natural-looking edging that keeps the grass in the path and out of the garden, and the wheel of the lawnmower can run right on top of the stones, eliminating the need for an edger or string-trimmer.

# Cape Cod Climbers—Plants for Arbors and Pergolas

Trumpet vine (*Campsis radicans*) is a fast-growing vine that thrives in poor, dry soil. It is valued for the bright, trumpet-shaped flowers that attract humming-birds, but because it spreads and is quite vigorous in good garden soils, some people find it too troublesome for the average landscape. Trumpet vine climbs to 30 feet high and more and blooms in late summer. Stem rootlets called hold-fasts bind it to posts, arbors, or build-ings.

Wisteria (*Wisteria floribunda, W. sinensis, W. frutescens*) is another very vigor-ous, sometimes invasive vine that is most suitable for large arbors. On smaller structures it should be frequently pruned. Japanese wisteria (*W. floribunda*) and Chinese wisteria (*W. sinensis*) are the species most frequently seen in nurseries, but the American wisteria (*W. frutescens*), less aggressive than the Chinese and Japanese varieties, is more widely of-fered.

Climbing roses are among the best flowers for smaller arbors and trellises. Because they bloom on new growth, climbing roses can be pruned every spring to control their size and keep plants from becoming too leggy. Roses need full sun, so they should be used on structures that receive at least five hours of direct sunshine, including the noon hour.

Clematis are wonderful vines, but be-cause they are prone to a fungal condi-tion called clematis wilt, they can take some time to get well established in Cape gardens. The fungi that cause wilt enter the plant through small wounds that in this area are frequently caused by windy weather. Once plants are well es-tablished, they are usually more resistant to wilt, but extended periods of wind and rain can occasionally cause even ma-ture plants to wilt. Fortunately, once in-fected stems are cut out and thrown away, the plant seems to recover and in future seasons may be problem-free. The old saying that clematis need "their heads in the sun and their feet in the shade" is not really true; if clematis are grown in organically amended soil and receive at least five hours of sunlight, they will do just fine.

Kiwi (*Actinidia* species) are vines na-tive to southwestern China. There are va-rieties of kiwi that bear fruit when a male and female plant are grown togeth-er, and other varieties that have variegat-ed leaves, especially on the male plants. With the exception of *Actinidia deliciosa*, the species of kiwi that produces the large fruits we find in supermarkets, these plants are perfectly hardy on Cape Cod and form dense foliage when grown on supports in part sun or filtered shade.

Magnolia vine (*Schisandra chinensis*) is a valuable vine for arbors in part-shade gardens. The flowers are cream-colored and small, but the edible fruit is a more showy red that is beautiful against the dark green foliage. Self-seeding can be somewhat of a problem with this other-wise maintenance-free vine.

Honeysuckle (*Lonicera* species) is fast-growing and most suitable for large trel-lises and arbors in full sun, but gardeners need to choose this plant carefully. Some varieties of honeysuckle are invasive, some are very prone to mildew, and oth-ers need frequent pruning to keep them from looking ratty. The woodbine honey-suckle, *Lonicera periclymenum* 'Belgica', is less prone to mildew and valued for repeat flowering and fragrance, but it can be more difficult to find than the mildew-prone variety called 'Goldflame'. Although honeysuckle will tolerate a half day of shade, it is more resistant to mildew if planted in a sunny area with good air circulation.

Climbing hydrangea (*Hydrangea anomala petiolaris*) is a slow-growing, styl-ish vine for sun or shade. The dark green leaves are handsome all summer, and es-tablished plants are covered with lacy white flowers in early summer. This vine climbs by twining and holdfasts, but it can take a few years to get going. Once settled, however, it can grow as much as 50 feet high. Even though it's a decidu-ous plant, climbing hydrangea is attrac-tive in all seasons because the exfoliating bark is interesting in the winter.

Hyacinth bean (*Dolichos lablab*) will grow between 10 and 15 feet high in one season, making it a good choice when a large annual vine is needed. Be-cause the stems, flowers, and seedpods are all purple, this plant is quite orna-mental. Grow hyacinth bean from seeds started indoors in late April and place the plants outdoors in late May. The vine is attractive on trellises, chain-link fences, or temporary bean teepees placed in full sun.

Morning glories (*Ipomoea purpurea* and others) are perhaps the most popular annual vines because they are fast-growing and their purple or blue flowers are so beautiful in late summer. Gardeners need to be careful not to treat their morning glories too generously, however, because this plant blooms best when kept on a lean diet. Poor soil, no fertilizer, and a minimal amount of water produce more flowers than highly fertile soil and regular watering.

Moonflower vine (*Ipomoea alba*) is a close relative of the morning glory that has large white flowers that open in the late afternoon. The blossoms remain open all night, attracting pollinating insects with a sweet fragrance that perfumes summer nights. Moonflowers grow quickly in hot weather, and the fluted, funnel-shaped flowers are about the size of a saucer. This is the perfect vine to grow near a patio, hot tub, or any other place where you are likely to be on a summer evening. Moonflowers can grow 10 feet or more in one season, and they do well in average garden soil.

Cardinal climber (*Ipomoea × multifida*) is another fast-growing annual *Ipomoea*, but its foliage, unlike that of the morning glory or moonflower, is fernlike and fine in texture. This *Ipomoea* also has much smaller, trumpet-shaped flowers that are bright red, a perfect contrast to the delicate green foliage. The plants grow to 8 feet or more and should be planted outdoors in late May or early June.

Black-eyed Susan vine (*Thunbergia alata*) has sweet, round-lobed flowers that are yellow, orange, or pink with dark centers. It is a small annual vine that is suitable for an obelisk, container garden, small trellis, or hanging basket. Plant black-eyed Susan vine in late May or early June, well after the chill has gone out of the sea breeze.

compact soil next to the walkway. Because moss usually arrives on its own, does not have to be fertilized or mowed, and is bright green in all seasons, many gardeners are thrilled when moss appears: it is the ultimate in low-maintenance landscaping.

Whether planting in sunny areas or in shade, Cape gardeners know that grouping plants by placing them in "puddles" of three or five of the same variety makes a garden most attractive. Repeating one or two of these groups in several places down the walkway becomes a way to unify the entire passageway.

# Man-made Structures

A beautiful garden isn't just a collection of annuals, perennials, shrubs, and trees. It is the synergy that results from a group of plants placed near buildings, archways, and other man-made structures that creates a lovely garden. Ornaments also play a role; when placed in and around a landscape, garden ornaments add the individual touches that make each garden unique.

Cape Cod gardeners love structures in the garden. Garden sheds with flower-filled window boxes, fences draped with rambling roses, and arbors covered with flowering vines are often included in the landscape.

## Arbors, Pergolas, and Outdoor Living Spaces

Arches and arbors can frame entrances and exits, provide transitions between indoor and outdoor living spaces, and create a shady retreat. Traditionally, an arbor is a structure that provides the same shade as a tree, and this is where the arbor gets its name. Modern arbors are often used to frame an opening in a fence or the gap in the hedge, and it's the perfect place to grow climbing roses, clematis, or small annual vines. Most of the time, arbors are not attached to a house.

A pergola is usually larger than an arbor. Pergolas were

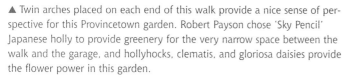

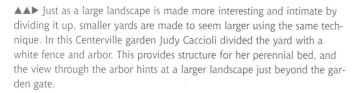

▲ Twin arches placed on each end of this walk provide a nice sense of perspective for this Provincetown garden. Robert Payson chose 'Sky Pencil' Japanese holly to provide greenery for the very narrow space between the walk and the garage, and hollyhocks, clematis, and gloriosa daisies provide the flower power in this garden.

▲▲▶ Just as a large landscape is made more interesting and intimate by dividing it up, smaller yards are made to seem larger using the same technique. In this Centerville garden Judy Caccioli divided the yard with a white fence and arbor. This provides structure for her perennial bed, and the view through the arbor hints at a larger landscape just beyond the garden gate.

▲▶ A twig arbor that supports a grapevine marks the passage between wild and tame in Susan Witzell's garden in Falmouth. Rustic arbors that frame a path leading into the woods are a clever way to visually hint that a natural area is, perhaps, a woodland garden.

▲◀ With an arbor, some vines, and comfortable furniture, Pat Dyke created the perfect Cape Cod summer place.

▲ Large groups of pots and boxes transform this plant collector's deck into an outdoor living space. People, plants, and hummingbirds happily gather in this container garden.

◀◀ Under the pergola in Sivert Johnston's garden, color is everything. The peach umbrella, yellow chair, blue hydrangea, green inkberry, and lavender *Nepeta* are a cheerful and festive combination. The chain draped over the pergola's frame and the imported ceramic elephant table suggest that this is the place where the world traveler's ship has pulled into Cape Cod for the summer.

◀ Morning glories are grown up the lattice at the back of the pergola, and a dwarf Alberta spruce adds structure to a bed of mixed annuals and perennials.

# Cape Containers—Plants for Pots and Boxes

*Scaevola*, sometimes called blue-fan flower, comes to us from New Zealand, and is one of the easiest annuals for all-summer color. Available with blue or white flowers, *Scaevola* cascades over the edges of containers and combines well with geraniums or yellow marguerites. To keep *Scaevola* thick and bushy, cut three or four of the stems back by half on a weekly basis, and grow it in full sun.

"Wave" petunias are sterile, so they do not need to be deadheaded in order to keep them blooming. In containers or in the ground, "Wave" petunias grow to 3 or 4 feet long, and, like *Scaevola*, they benefit from periodic pruning of the stems. Plant these annuals in full or part sun with some time-release fertilizer and they will produce colorful flowers all summer and into September.

Million bells (*Callibrachoa* hybrids) look like miniature petunias, and they come in a variety of clear colors that grow well in sun or part sun. Million bells grow 12 to 18 inches high and wide, so they are especially appropriate for window boxes and smaller containers. Because it does well in cool temperatures, this annual is perfect for refreshing pots and boxes in the fall.

'Red Riding Hood' *Mandevilla*, a short variety of the *Mandevilla* vine, produces bright pinkish-red flowers that need no deadheading. Formerly in the genus *Dipladenia* but now grouped with the *Mandevillas*, this annual grows 18 to 20 inches tall and flowers all summer.

The glossy green foliage is as attractive as the flowers, and the plant combines well with Persian shield, *Scaevola*, licorice plant, and million bells in a mixed-annual container.

Impatiens can't be beat for season-long flowering and ease. Whether the common *Impatiens walleriana* that are sold in six-packs, the large-flowering New Guineas, the cascading "Fanfare Series," or the peach-and-yellow "Fusion Series" (the last two in the Simply Beautiful group of plants), impatiens are low-maintenance and reliable. They are also more sun-tolerant than most people realize, and they flower best when they receive at least three hours of direct sunlight. Although they do not like going completely dry, impatiens are prone to crown rot when frequently hit with water.

"Profusion Series" zinnias are short, bushy plants that produce small zinnia flowers all summer. These annuals can be tidied by deadheading, but even when the older flowers are left on the plant, they continue to bloom. Because of their compact size, these zinnias are perfect for containers, window boxes, or the front of the flower garden. Like other zinnias, the "Profusion Series" plants need full sun and don't like wet leaves: water them by placing a hose or watering can underneath the foliage so the moisture goes directly to the soil.

Purple oxalis (*Oxalis regnellii* 'Atropurpurea') has rich, dark purple leaves and

delicate pink flowers floating above the plant on thin stems. It is the perfect plant for containers in part or full shade, and is a great companion to begonias and asparagus fern.

Licorice plant (*Helichrysum petiolare*) will weave its silver stems in and out of a container, but it should be used sparingly because a single plant can quickly dominate an entire small window box or flowerpot. Licorice plant grows well in full sun or part shade, and it is especially attractive when combined with plants that have purple foliage, such as Persian shield or purple heart (*Setcreasea pallida*).

'Silver Falls' Dichondra (*Dichondra argentea* 'Silver Falls') is another silver foliage plant, but this cascading annual has small round leaves that look almost metallic. 'Silver Falls' can be used to cascade over the edge of walls or window boxes, and it is also attractive when planted as an annual groundcover. 'Silver Falls' *Dichondra* is both heat- and drought-tolerant.

Persian shield (*Strobilanthes dyerianus*) is a subshrub in areas where it is hardy, but it is a striking foliage plant for containers in northern climates. The purple leaves of Persian shield have a metallic iridescence that adds to their dramatic look and complements silver annuals such as licorice plant or 'Silver Falls' *Dichondra*.

invented as a way to connect two buildings with a shady "hallway" so that people wouldn't have to walk in the hot sun when traveling from one place to another. Pergolas create outdoor living spaces, providing shade and structure as well as a strong support for larger vines.

Larger arbors and pergolas can define outdoor living spaces, creating a shady, open-air room. They provide the perfect setting for furniture and groups of plant-filled containers.

## The Garden Shed

Although increasing storage space is the primary purpose for adding a shed to a landscape, most gardeners also appreciate the substance and charm that these storage structures add to the garden. Cape garden sheds are usually

built to match the style of the house, so many of them are covered with shingles. Colorful paint applied to the door and shutters can add to the appeal of these miniature houses, and for some Cape Codders, a large shed can even evolve into a guest cabin, workshop, or studio space. In this case,

▲◀ As Nancy Walsh demonstrates, a shed can be as ornamental as it is functional.

▲ When Dave Rogers was building this storage shed, he and his wife, Judy, decided that the developing outbuilding was too good to waste on tools and flowerpots, so they decided to turn the structure into a sleeping cabin. Purposefully lacking plumbing and electricity, the building has large screened windows and is furnished with a bed and night table. Dave says that sleeping with no lights or hum of electrical equipment, and waking up to the singing of the birds, is "absolutely magical." Growing on the corner of this quiet cabin is a climbing hydrangea.

▲ The bold use of color can transform something functional, such as a gate, a wheelbarrow, or a chair, here in Sivert Johnston's garden, into a garden ornament.

◄ Ric Ide displays his work throughout this Provincetown garden, where he periodically changes the placement of his ceramic sculptures. This twist of pottery finials on copper stakes adds a touch of height, color, and movement to these hillside plantings.

▲◄◄ My mother, Jan Albertson, was an interior designer, and she used to say that if there is a visual problem or difficulty, you should *accentuate* it. This area was problematic because it was bordered on two sides with asphalt, so most of the time it was hot and dry. Fairly regularly, however, the area would flood. Not only would the plants be under water for a day, but as the puddle receded, it took all the organic amendments and mulch with it. Most of the plants placed in this area died, so the area was usually a stretch of bare sand. Pot Man to the rescue! This ornament fills the sandy spot and draws the eye away from the bare spot.

◄◄◄ This gardener knows that one of the most important things to take into the garden is a sense of humor.

◄◄ A wire clamming basket makes the perfect Cape Cod garden ornament. Filled with seashells, glass net floats, or blue-and-white ceramic balls, it can be placed in the garden wherever a touch of color or whimsy is needed.

◄ A collection of terra-cotta flower pots can be used ornamentally in a variety of situations. In the Cotés' garden they soften the hard edge of a painted cement wall.

▲ Lobster buoys on Beverly Lopes's garden shed provide a summery scene viewed from the vegetable garden.

▲▶ Garden ornaments don't have to be formal or expensive; the addition of paper lanterns makes Pat Dyke's garden look like a celebration.

▶ Nancy Walsh is an expert at combining odd and vintage items to create areas of interest in her South Yarmouth garden. Her displays make reference to rural America and are often humorous as well. This collection shows how a group of items makes a more powerful ornamentation than one item alone.

▶▶ Pat Dyke combines her love of poetry and gardens by writing a section from Solomon's "Song of Songs" on white ceramic tiles.

the building really is a small dwelling, complete with everything but plumbing.

The flowers that spill from a shed's window box are often visible from the house, and flowering shrubs, climbing roses, or vines are usually planted around the building. No matter what a shed's function, watering cans, pots, or other garden tools are frequently used to embellish the building and the garden that surrounds it.

## Absolutely Ornamental

Ornaments serve several functions in the garden. The solidity of their composition contrasts well with the finer textures of foliage, and they can add color wherever it's needed. Garden ornaments reflect the taste and personality of the gardener and can also provide a touch of whimsy.

Cape Cod gardeners also use ornaments to fill empty areas where a plant may have died, or where the soil is so compact, dry, or sandy that few plants will survive. Objects are the perfect fillers in such situations, turning a problem space into an attractive accent for the landscape.

Antiques make good garden ornaments because they provide a sense of timelessness and familiarity, and items related to the area where the garden is located supply an

added sense of place. For this reason, ornaments that have a seaside theme are popular on Cape Cod.

Lobster buoys and traps, clam baskets, miniature lighthouses, and seashells are common ornaments for Cape gardens, and many Cape gardeners are aware that the size of the object may dictate how it is used in the landscape. Small ornaments are best when used sparingly, or when positioned in clusters. When ornaments that are under a foot tall and wide are placed in several locations in the garden, they make a garden look cluttered. But if they are gathered together and arranged in groups of three, five, or seven, they become a *collection* instead of a muddle of dots.

## Water in the Garden

It isn't surprising that those who garden in an area surrounded by water frequently choose to bring that element into their landscapes. On Cape Cod, water gardens of all sorts continue to increase in popularity. From small fountains to large ponds, water features can add sound, color, and movement to the garden.

Whether it is from a waterfall, fountain, or in-pond sprinkler, there is something soothing about the sound of trickling water. And because the element of sound is as important as a water feature's appearance, it is usually located near a patio, porch, or other sitting area where the motion of the water can easily be seen and heard.

# A Passion for Plants

The love of horticulture affects Cape gardeners in a variety of ways. For some it manifests itself as an interest in a particular species of plant; others are challenged to grow tender or tropical plants that are not normally hardy in this region. And then there are those who will try to grow practically anything.

When gardeners love hydrangeas, heather, or roses, for example, they often collect as many varieties of these plants as they can find. From there, a passion for plants usually moves from purchase to propagation, and soon the plant enthusiast begins to root cuttings and germinate seeds.

Garden lovers don't stop with selections they have culti-

▲ Raindrop diamonds hang from an old-fashioned bleeding heart *(Dicentra spectabilis)* in a spring garden.

▲◀◀ There is little doubt that Cape Cod gardeners love water gardens. In the pond and around its perimeter, John Sullivan's garden is a constantly changing celebration of color.

▲◀ The pond in the back of Vern and Mary Lopez's house looks cool and serene. In addition to perennial aquatic plants, Mary placed a variety of potted tropical plants in the water every summer.

◀ Perennials for pond margins and potted tropical plants combine to create a verdant, leafy border at the edges of Arthur Clark's pond.

▲ Arthur Clark divided his backyard into thirds; the center section is a lawn bordered by flower beds, and the sides are large pools where water lilies and other water-garden plants flourish.

◄ Harry Bowen's garden is filled with several types of heath and heather, in addition to many varieties of shrubs and trees.

▶ Paul Miskovsky, a landscape designer, used the boulders that a glacier dropped on his East Falmouth property to create a lovely dual waterfall. Designed by Paul and installed by Miskovsky Landscaping, this garden contains numerous specimen shrubs and trees, along with perennials and annuals, all chosen and placed with an eye for foliage color and texture. The movement of the water and the interplay of light on the plants create a garden that is simultaneously soothing and energetic.

▲ John Sullivan likes his plants big, bold, and colorful, so in addition to the perennial black-eyed Susans and hardy hibiscus, he fills his beds with tender annuals such as canna and *Alocasia*.

▶ In August and September three of the author's favorite plants are looking their best. 'Final Touch' daylilies bloom later than most, and are a clear coral pink with a greenish-yellow throat. 'Fusion Glow' impatiens are about 18 inches high in late summer, and their peachy-yellow flowers echo the tints of the daylilies. *Calamintha nepetoides* is a contrast in texture and flower color— the lesser calamint has dainty lavender to white flowers and fine foliage.

▶▶ Mary Lopez was a Cape Cod gardener who was passionate about plants. She was an accomplished propagator of primroses, which were planted under the shade of pines, oaks, and rhododendrons.

vated, however: self-seeded plants are also prized and often allowed to roam from bed to bed on a property. Biennials such as foxglove, *Verbascum*, and money plant will move around a property, growing one year, blooming the next, and scattering seed before dying. Although many home landscapers don't want such short-lived, traveling plants because they are unpredictable and often need to be edited or moved, passionate gardeners usually appreciate self-seeders on their own terms. Indeed, for many Cape gardeners, the problem is finding enough space to grow all the plants that they have propagated along with those that are self-sown.

Space is also an issue when it comes to raising plants in pots. Where do you keep them until they are large enough to place in the ground, and where do you store still-potted plants through the winter? Gardeners become as ingenious when it comes to housing their collections as they are industrious in growing the plants.

Orchids are hung on the sides of sheds, and back decks become container gardens. Driveways hold potted nursery stock, and baby perennials are placed under the shade of trees. Hoop houses, greenhouses, and plastic plant huts are erected if there is room, tropical plants are brought into the house, and tender perennials or shrubs are pulled into garages and sheds. For Cape Cod gardeners, the old saying "Where there is the will, there is a way" is especially apt, for they will find a means to grow the plants that capture their fancy.

# Chapter 4

# CAPE COD GARDEN STYLE

I t is the ocean that defines Cape Cod; the sea surrounds us and draws people to this region. When you are on Cape Cod, you are never more than a twenty-minute drive from the shore. The entire area is affected by the sea. Even those who live several miles from the coastline receive the off-ocean winds that keep the Cape cooler in the summer and warmer in the winter.

The sea breeze that tempers our climate presents some challenges to Cape gardeners. Because the wind moves across a cold ocean in April and May, spring can be cruel on Cape Cod. Annuals and vegetables that prefer warmer weather can't be planted before the end of May, and damp, raw weather often keeps gardeners indoors until June.

Cold spring winds can damage plants, often doing more harm than the below-freezing winter temperatures. Cape gardeners may see plants such as their beloved hydrangeas break dormancy in March, only to have the newly emerging leaves zapped by frigid winds in April.

Gardeners on Cape Cod quickly learn not to put annuals in the garden too soon, and to plant hydrangeas where they are sheltered from the breezes. Those who garden near the coast frequently use fences or hedges to break the wind and protect flower gardens; even a small fence shields tender plants from icy gusts.

The cold spring winds aren't the only problem for Cape gardeners. Although the off-ocean winds cool Cape landscapes through the summer and warm the region into the fall, autumn also brings coastal storms. Windy, rainy weather can knock tall plants to the ground, so some gardeners avoid placing delicate or very tall plants in exposed locations.

Because some plants withstand salt better than others, those who plant exposed seaside gardens may need to consider using salt-tolerant plants. Native plants such as

▲ Meg McCarthy's garden is filled with Cape Cod favorites, such as shrub roses, *Gaura*, and hydrangeas. This Oyster Pond garden was designed and planted by Edson Eldredge of North Chatham Landscapes.

◄ Looking down the length of this perennial border at an original cranberry house, you could be gazing through time at a view of old Cape Cod.

A long row of hydrangeas makes a classic Cape Cod hedge at the edge of the McCarthys' lawn.

bayberry, beach plum, and bearberry grow well near the ocean, and junipers, yews, and privet also tolerate both salt and wind. Salt spray may not be only detrimental to plants, however. There are those who believe that the slight amount of salt in the air keeps roses resistant to leaf diseases such as mildew, so the plants do better near the ocean than they do farther inland.

*Rosa rugosa*, often called the beach rose, is frequently planted in Cape landscapes and grows wild along the shore. This rugged rose is so widespread on Cape beaches that people frequently think it is native to the area. The beach rose is a wash-ashore from the orient, however. Legend has it that sailors carried the fleshy *Rosa rugosa* seedpods, called rosehips, on long voyages. Because the hips are high in vitamin C, they were eaten to prevent scurvy. Once the edible portion of the pod was eaten, the tale goes, the seeds were tossed overboard, eventually washing up on the beach and germinating there.

Although there is no way of knowing if this story is true, it is undeniable that the beach rose flourishes here. Rugosa roses grow so well in pure sand that they are almost invasive on Cape beaches and in the garden. Although they may seem to be the perfect plant for dry, sandy slopes, *Rosa rugosa* can be problematic in the landscape in several respects.

The beach rose quickly grows out of bounds and is prone to invading neighboring lawns and flowerbeds. They don't compete very successfully with weeds, however. Because they are rather open and don't shade the ground, it's easy for weed seeds to germinate underneath their branches. Those who grow *Rosa rugosa* find it difficult to control wild plants growing among the thorny stems, and patches of beach rose easily become filled with weeds.

An alternative plant for dry, sandy areas is American beach grass (*Ammophila breviligulata*), the two- to three-foot grass that grows near the shore. Many ornamental grasses are mistakenly called "beach grass" on Cape Cod, but this *Ammophila* is the true native grass that has the ability to thrive in pure sand and survive coastal conditions.

American beach grass grows from New England to North Carolina on the East Coast, and it's found in other areas of the country as well. Because the plant has the abili-

Ann Charlesworth chose the perfect plants to brighten this seaside garden. The yellow flowers of lady's mantle (*Alchemilla mollis*) and yarrow (*Achillea*) are bright even on a foggy day.

▲ An old compass pedestal from the bridge of a ship spends its retirement as a garden ornament. The low wall frames the garden nicely and protects this perennial bed from off-ocean winds.

▲▶ Pink evening primrose *(Oenethera speciosa)* and blue peach-leaf campanula *(Campanula persicifolia)* add color to the alluring view from Susan Ambrose's garden in Barnstable.

ty to continue to grow even as wind-blown sand buries it, American beach grass plays an important role in the stabilization of dunes. Its very name, *Ammophila*, comes from the Greek words *ammos* for "sand" and *fileiu* for "love." This plant adores the beach, so some Cape gardeners wisely choose beach grass as the perfect plant for dry, sandy areas.

Other grasses are also well liked on Cape Cod, partly because they are reminiscent of the plants that grow on the shore. Several varieties of *Miscanthus*, sometimes called maiden or silver grass, are especially popular, although there are concerns that *Miscanthus sinensis* self-seeds prolifically enough to be invasive. The named cultivars such as 'Morning Light' seem to set seed much later than the species plant, so at present there is not as much apprehension that these varieties will become problematic.

Fountain grass (*Pennisetum alopecuroides*) is shorter than *Miscanthus*, and gardeners favor this plant for its graceful, rounded form and foxtail seed heads. Like all varieties of *Miscanthus*, fountain grass thrives in full sun, tolerates drought, and is available in a range of sizes.

Although *Pennisetum alopecuroides* is fully hardy on the Cape, red fountain grass (*Pennisetum setaceum* 'Rubrum') does not live through the winter in this climate. Gardeners still love this grass for its dark burgundy leaves and pink foxtail blooms, and it is frequently planted in gardens and containers as an annual.

Hakone grass is also prized for its flowing texture and foliage color, and this plant reliably returns from year to year. Although it is not as evocative of the seashore or as drought-tolerant as many grasses, it grows well in part-shade or full sun. Two varieties of *Hakonechloa macra*, 'Aureola' and 'All Gold', are the most commonly planted varieties because their bright yellow foliage adds color to the garden from April to November.

The smart gardener will amend the soil well when planting Hakone grass; in fact, soil amendment is the key to success for most gardening on Cape Cod. Although plants such as American beach grass, rugosa rose, bayberry, and beach plum will grow in pure sand, other plants need or-

ganic matter added to the native soil at planting time and on an ongoing basis.

Sand does not hold on to moisture or nutrients well enough for most plants to thrive, and most gardeners on Cape Cod have sandy properties. Many add loam to their soil, but the regular addition of organics such as compost or composted manure is still a necessity to keep established plants healthy.

Such organic materials are mixed into the soil before plants are put in place, and they are used annually to top-dress the area around established plants. Because the microorganisms that keep soil healthy and help plants to grow

▲ Cape Codders love ornamental grasses for their ease of maintenance and their soft texture. Grasses add motion to the garden, and here, in a Cotuit garden planted by Thomas Norton, they evoke the grasses that grow wild at the beach.

▶ Low fountain grasses (*Pennisetum alopecuroides* 'Hameln') are in their glory at the same time the blue-mist shrub (*Caryopteris × clandonensis*) blooms in this West Falmouth garden.

▶▶ Will Clarke has created a flower-filled, casual garden for this bay-side garden using several clumps of *Miscanthus* and other grasses along with flowering shrubs and perennials.

depend on decaying organic matter, regular applications of this material are necessary.

Cape gardeners with sandy soil may value the good drainage that this type of earth provides, but they need to add a layer of compost or composted manure annually, and they often apply an annual layer of mulch as well. This constant amendment of sandy soils from the top down, which is the system nature uses in wild areas, is the key to success for growing beautiful gardens on Cape Cod.

## Classic Cape Cod

If you ask people which plants they associate with Cape Cod, the answer is usually "roses and hydrangeas." From Woods Hole to Provincetown, the Cape is in bloom with roses in June and hydrangeas in July and August. It is difficult to find a garden on Cape Cod that does not have one or both of these plants, and with good reason. Roses and hydrangeas thrive here.

Roses proclaim the beginning of summer on the Cape. Climbing roses scramble over fences and arbors, shrub roses

## Surviving Sandy Soils

When planting in sandy soils, amend entire beds, not just the immediate area around a single plant. As the plant grows, its root system will spread wide; if the roots grow out of the amended area into the sand beyond, the plant is likely to weaken just as it is maturing.

As time goes on, soil amendments break down. Nature amends soils continually when leaves and branches fall around a plant and decompose in place. Since gardeners clean up fallen foliage and other plant debris, they need to amend the soil with an annual application of organic matter, placed on the surface of the soil. Composted or partly composted leaves are good soil amendments, as are pine needles. These do not make soil more acidic. Seaweed is also a good amendment, and it does not need to be rinsed before putting it in the garden or compost pile. Compost and composted manure can be purchased in bags or in bulk from most garden centers, and

a one-inch layer is all that is needed for established gardens. Soil amendments can be applied right over any mulch that remains in the garden.

Top-dressing the garden with mulch helps retain moisture in sandy soils, and the decomposing mulch is a helpful amendment for all soil types. When applied in early spring, mulch prevents the germination of most weed seeds. Keep mulch away from the stems of shrubs, trees, perennials, and annuals, because it can make these areas damp enough to promote diseases.

Organic fertilizers are perfect for Cape Cod gardens because they provide nutrients that are released slowly. This is how Mother Nature fertilizes plants in the wild, after all, and she's been gardening far longer than we have. Keep the "fast-food fertilizers" on hand for the annuals, or for nutrition emergencies, but use organic fertilizers for routine fertilization of perennials, shrubs, and trees.

Emulate nature when watering gardens as well as when fertilizing them: water deeply, but water less often. When lawns are watered too frequently, fungal diseases and the growth of moss and bent grass are encouraged. When shrubs are frequently splashed with water, the ideal conditions for leaf-spot fungus are created, and when perennials are kept too damp, the plants can die from crown rot. Everything in the landscape, including the lawn, will grow well on an inch of water a week, delivered in one rainfall or sprinkling. Water gardens with a sprinkler until a rain gauge measures an inch. If your garden is mulched, you will not have to water again for a week in all but extremely hot, sunny weather. If you have an automatic sprinkler, be sure to turn it off if there has been rain within one week. Keeping automatic systems on during rainy periods squanders a most precious resource.

---

bloom in foundation plantings and perennial borders, and hybrid teas fill the rose gardens. Rugosa roses bloom on the beach and even the wild and invasive *Rosa multiflora* fills Cape Cod with fragrance in early summer.

Many roses continue to bloom into the summer and fall as well; others produce colorful rosehips in autumn. It is typical for Cape houses to have a trellis where the flowers of 'New Dawn' or 'Climbing America' show off against gray shingles. Numerous other varieties of roses bloom in sunny gardens, often growing along with other shrubs and perennials.

Unlike the roses, hydrangeas prefer a bit of shade. This

Cape favorite will tolerate full sun and even seashore conditions, but the flowers last longer if they are shaded from the afternoon sun. There are several species of hydrangeas, but the big-leaf hydrangeas (*Hydrangea macrophylla*) are popular plants that include those with lacecap flowers and pompom flowers.

It is the pom-poms, or mophead hydrangeas, that are arguably Cape Cod's favorite shrub. Mopheads are also called hortensias, named in honor of Hortense, the daughter of the eighteenth-century botanist the prince of Nassau. Mopheads have large, rounded flower heads that usually bloom from early summer well into fall. Often their flowers are so

▲ Perhaps Cape residents love shingled houses because they seem to be the perfect backdrop for roses.

Pink 'Bonica' and peach 'Royal Sunset' roses catch the morning sun in the Rose Man's garden.

The most popular climbing rose on Cape Cod just might be 'New Dawn'. Although it blooms for only two weeks in June, it is a disease-resistant, strong climber, and it's hard not to fall in love with the soft pink flowers.

A section of Irwin Ehrenreich's garden proves that you can never have too many roses.

vent the flowers from falling to the ground, especially when they are wet from rain. Some hortensia blooms are white, but most are shades of pink or blue, depending on soil pH.

For many years the 'Nikko Blue' mophead has been king on Cape Cod, but many new or different varieties are becoming available every year. 'Nikko Blue' is filled with pale blue or pale pink flowers, but it grows to six feet tall and wide, making it too large for some locations. Although 'Nikko Blue' has been a favorite Cape shrub, those with smaller landscapes need not despair. Other varieties such as 'Mathilda Gutges', 'Meritt's Supreme', and 'Hortensis compacta' stay shorter and are more suitable for foundation plantings or smaller gardens. And there are several miniature types, such as 'Pia' and 'Forever Pink', that grow only two feet tall.

Varieties such as 'Alpengluhen', also called 'Glowing Embers', and 'Meritt's Supreme' bloom dark pink in alkaline soils and dark purple in acidic soils, but some pink varieties do not change color readily. Cape gardeners enjoy experimenting with flower color by adding sulfur or aluminum sulfate to make soil more acidic or lime to make it neutral or alkaline, or using some of each on different sides of the plant to create a shrub with multicolor blossoms.

Lacecap hydrangeas differ from the mopheads in that their flowers are a striking mix of small, fertile flowers in the center surrounded by a ring of larger, sterile blooms. Sometimes these two components are different colors, and they do indeed resemble lace.

Like the mopheads, lacecap hydrangeas usually bloom on the previous year's growth so they shouldn't be severely pruned (see "Hydrangea Happy," below). The lacecaps are less sun-tolerant than the hortensias, and their flowers last longer if they are sited where they receive morning sun but afternoon shade.

New varieties of hydrangeas are released yearly, so the palette of these Cape favorites continues to grow. Plants that produce flowers on old *and* new growth, such as 'Endless Summer' and 'Blushing Bride', are valuable for those who want to place a hydrangea in a colder, more exposed lo-

cation. New plants that stay shorter, such as the 'Little Lamb' variety of peegee hydrangea (*Hydrangea paniculata*) and the 'Pee Wee' oakleaf (*Hydrangea quercifolia*), please those with small gardens, and those that have flowers that start out or turn green, such as 'Limelight' and 'Queen of Pearls', please flower arrangers. On Cape Cod there is truly a hydrangea for every garden.

There is also a rhododendron for every landscape on the Cape, and this is probably the region's favorite evergreen shrub. Rhodies are used for screening, foundation plantings, and mixed borders. From the early blooming small-leaf varieties such as 'PJM', 'Olga', and 'PJM Aglo' to the large-leaf plants that bloom anywhere from late spring to midsummer, the rhododendron grows happily in the Cape's well-drained, naturally acidic soils. Short varieties such as the "Yak" series (*Rhododendron yakushimanum* or *R. degronianum* ssp. *yakushimanum*) are well suited for growing near houses or with perennials and dwarf conifers, and tall types such as *Rhododendron maximum* 'Roseum Elegans' and 'Anna Rose Whitney' grow to be tall and wide enough for use as screening.

Small-leaf rhododendrons are often confused with azaleas. In fact, all azaleas are rhododendrons, but they are subgenera of this genus. In general, rhododendrons have larger, leathery leaves, flowers with ten or more stamens, and thick branches. Azaleas have small, pointed leaves with small hairs on the underside, flowers with five stamens, and brittle, twiggy branches.

Although azaleas are also rhododendrons, they need a

▲▶ 'Nikko Blue' hydrangeas make beautiful companions to July-blooming daylilies in Barbara Stewart's garden.

▲▶▶ Given a soil with neutral pH, *Hydrangea* 'Ami Pasquier' will begin blooming with cream-colored petals that change to lilac and mauve as the flowers mature.

▶ *Hydrangea* 'Mathilda Gutges' is a shorter variety with dark lavender-blue flowers. Because most hydrangeas do well in gardens that receive some sun and some shade, they combine nicely with hostas, which like the same growing conditions.

Lacecap hydrangeas have a group of small, fertile flowers that are surrounded by large, infertile flowers. Like other big-leaf hydrangeas, lacecaps bloom on the previous year's growth and their blooms last longer when planted in part shade.

bit more tending to than the larger-leaf varieties. Regular applications of organic matter to the surface of the soil and pruning immediately after bloom are necessary to keep evergreen azaleas thick and healthy on Cape Cod. The deciduous varieties seem to fare better in sandy soils than the evergreens do, however, and the bright orange- and yellow-flowering Exbury azaleas and lavender-blooming Korean azaleas grow well here.

Highly scented deciduous azaleas, such as the varieties 'Lemon Drop' and 'Lollipop', and the native swamp azalea (*Rhododendron viscosum*) are prized for their fragrance. In fact, 'Lemon Drop' is especially treasured because it blooms in July, when most people are outdoors and can enjoy its perfume.

Other Cape favorites include the wild lady's slipper orchid (*Cypripedium acaule*), which appears in undisturbed areas in May, and the kousa dogwood (*Cornus kousa*), a mid-size tree that is usually smothered with flowers in June.

# Hydrangea Happy

### Tips for Growing Cape Cod's Favorite Shrub

Take the "hydra" part of their name seriously: hydrangeas are not drought-tolerant. Amend the soil well with compost when planting, and apply two inches of mulch around the shrubs every spring. Water hydrangeas deeply every few days; do not water daily because frequent splashing with water will foster black spot on the foliage.

Most white-flowering hydrangeas, such as varieties of peegee, 'Annabelle', and 'White Dome', form flowers on new growth, so they can be pruned hard in the spring if necessary. In fact, in cold winters Annabelle may die to the ground, but it will dependably grow back and bloom in midsummer.

Most blue- or pink-flowering hydrangeas form flower buds on old growth, so they should never be pruned very much. Even the newer varieties such as 'Endless Summer' form flowers on both old *and* new growth, so a hard pruning, or very cold winter, will result in fewer flowers the following season. For the best floral display, prune hydrangeas in the late spring by first removing all deadwood, and then cleaning up the top of the shrub by cutting just above the first or second pair of live buds you come to, moving from the top down. Because the canes will grow their full height in one season, it is pointless to try to make a hydrangea smaller. The only pruning this plant usually needs is the removal of deadwood and any weak or oddly shaped canes, but congested, older shrubs can be renewed by cutting a third of the oldest canes to ground level.

Hydrangea color is often a mystery for Cape gardeners, but a hydrangea's color is simply a matter of variety and soil pH. It is aluminum in the soil that turns hydrangea flowers blue, but it's the acidity of the soil that makes the intake of aluminum possible. Those varieties of hydrangea flowers that can be blue or pink (some don't change color) will be blue in acid soils and pink in alkaline soils. Dark pink varieties will often turn purple when grown in acidic soil, but a pale flower will always be pale, be it blue or pink. To keep hydrangeas pink, add lime to the area every fall and spring. To turn hydrangeas blue, use an acidifying fertilizer or aluminum sulfate. Just don't overdo the fertilizer or the aluminum; too much will burn your plants and create an imbalanced soil.

If a hydrangea doesn't bloom, it's usually because of one or more of the following reasons. Because mophead hydrangeas bloom on the previous year's growth, they won't flower if they've been cut to the ground. If the temperature goes below zero in the winter, or if an early warm spell is followed by cold spring winds, the germ of the flower on hydrangea canes can be killed, the result being few—or no—blooms the following summer. Too much shade or close proximity to a lawn that's been given applications of high-nitrogen fertilizer can also cause hydrangeas not to bloom. In fact, studies show that overfertilized hydrangeas don't bloom as well as those that are kept on a leaner diet.

Support floppy hydrangeas with bamboo canes. Place an upright cane of bamboo in the center of the shrub, and then stick five or more around the edges of the plant, pushing them into the soil at the same angle that the hydrangea stems grow. Be sure that the bamboo is about a foot shorter than the top of the stems; if the supports are too tall they will show, and if they are too short the stems will fall over after a rain, when the flowers are heavy. After all the bamboo canes are firmly in the ground, run a cord from the center cane to each of the other bamboo canes, so that they are all supporting each other. Finally, run a cord around the entire plant to contain the heavy branches. The best time to stake a hydrangea, or any plant for that matter, is *before* it needs it. If you see many flowers forming on your plant, and the stems have fallen to the ground in the past, put the support system in early. Hydrangeas that are frequently watered and fertilized will have weaker stems that are prone to flopping.

## Cape Cottage Style

Many gardeners find that a gray-shingled Cape Cod–style home almost demands a cottage-style garden. Perfected in England, this form of garden includes flowering shrubs and perennials planted in wide beds in an informal, free-flowing manner. Although some of the plants that an Eng-

▲ The creamy white flowers of a kousa dogwood (*Cornus kousa*) appear at the start of the summer season on Cape Cod. This small tree does well in this region, and it is valued for its decorative seedpods and its long-lasting summer blooms.

◄ Pink lady's slipper orchids are a coveted plant for Cape gardeners; they grow best in the wild and should always remain untouched when they appear. The lady's slipper (*Cypripedium acaule*) is an endangered wildflower and does not transplant well. Lady's slippers grow with the cooperation of beneficial bacteria that are in the soil.

lish cottage garden contains, such as perennial geraniums and lady's mantle, do well on Cape Cod, others, such as delphiniums and hollyhocks, are a bit more challenging here.

The difficulties of some traditional cottage garden plants aside, Cape gardeners have developed their own style of cottage garden that includes flowering shrubs and annuals in addition to perennial plants. Although the classic English-style cottage garden looks a bit wild, when done well it is one of the most high-maintenance gardens you can plant.

Many of the traditional cottage garden plants, such as foxgloves (*Digitalis purpurea*), rose campion (*Lychnis coronaria*), and *Verbascum* are self-seeding biennials. In order to

▲ A flower-filled cottage garden is the ideal landscaping for this brick walkway and decoratively shingled house. Mary and Eric Beck have planted their cottage garden using a mix of hydrangeas, annuals, and perennials.

keep the garden looking good, these plants often need to be edited or moved. Although Cape gardeners often use these in their gardens, some opt to include less traditional but lower-maintenance perennials and flowering shrubs in their cottage gardens.

Russian sage (*Perovskia atriplicifolia*), Stokes' aster (*Stokesia laevis*), Nippon daisies (*Nipponanthemum nipponicum*), and daylilies (*Hemerocallis*) are some of the lower-maintenance perennials that Cape gardeners use in their cottage-style plantings. Annuals such as 'Blue Horizon' ageratum, dahlias, and *Scaevola* provide color all summer, and flowering shrubs such as weigela, hydrangea, *Caryopteris*, and rose of Sharon are easily grown. Shrub roses like 'Bonica', 'The Fairy', 'Knockout', and the Simplicity series are frequently added to the mix, producing a charming Cape Cod cottage garden.

## Summer Is the Season

Cape gardens are often appealing twelve months a year. Gardeners on Cape Cod, just like gardeners the world over, plant their flowerbeds and landscapes with an eye toward year-round interest. But summer is *the* season on the Cape,

▲ David Kirchner and Scott Warner wanted their front yard to be filled with a cottage garden, so they've used a  preponderance of perennials, with some annuals added for bridge color through the season. In late July the garden is filled with white *Gaura*, purple *Verbena bonariensis*, yellow *Patrinia scabiosifolia*, white Shasta daisies, pink summer phlox, and an edging of annual blue ageratum.

▶ Gordon Gaskill designed and maintained this Provincetown garden for Suzanne Sinaiko Buka. Suzanne was an artist, and before this garden was planted, she took Gordon to Monet's garden in France for inspiration. Although both the artist and the plantsman are no longer with us, this garden remains the ultimate example of Cape Cod cottage style.

and because the early fall is so warm, summer weather and summer gardens are delightful from mid-June through September.

Many houses fly flags or red, white, and blue buntings throughout the entire season, making it seem as if the Fourth of July lasts all summer. Garden furnishings such as benches, hammocks, and picnic tables invite everyone to enjoy some shade and the sea breeze on the hottest days and the lawns and flower gardens during dry, sunny weather. And colorful annuals fill whisky barrels, flowerpots, window boxes, and gardens.

▲◄ Cottage gardens are frequently a cheerful tumble of flowers, herbs, and vegetables, and this is the look captured in the raised beds of the McGuinness-Wright garden in Provincetown. Mike Wright created the found-wood sculpture that adorns the back fence.

▲▲ Carol P. Duffy has designed and planted this pleasing cottage garden in Osterville using traditional favorites such as hollyhocks, shrub roses, and Shasta daisies. Like many Cape gardeners, she also includes several ornamental grasses and annuals.

▲ Summer phlox and biennial *Verbascum* are traditional cottage garden plants. Here they grow near the bamboo poles that will support dahlias later in the season.

▲ Oxeye daisies, veronica, and basket-of-gold are just a few of the perennials that mingle in this garden.

▲▶ Oriental poppies, lavender, and pink yarrow combine with the daisies to make an impressionist painting of a garden in June.

Cape Cod landscapes usually include patios, decks, or groupings of furniture on the lawn, placed to encourage everyone to stop and enjoy the warm weather. Even those who don't live lives of leisure create outdoor living spaces to better enjoy their landscape when time allows. On the beach or in the garden, all of Cape Cod celebrates the summer season.

## A Sense of Place

How is a Cape Cod garden different from a garden in other parts of Massachusetts? Are they unlike gardens in Madison, Wisconsin, or Santa Barbara, California? Gardeners on the Cape often express the desire to have a unique landscape, one that gives the immediate impression that it is located on Cape Cod, and not in Boston, Madison, or Santa Barbara. It is of value, many feel, to be in a garden and know that this garden is located on the Cape.

A garden's sense of place is primarily derived from the

▲▲ Gordon Gaskill loved *Verbena bonariensis*, and with good reason. This tall, tender annual self-seeds, so even if the parent plant doesn't make it through the winter, the seedlings provide enough flowers to please gardeners and butterflies.

▲ In September the delphiniums that were cut down in early summer return to bloom again.

▲▶ The walk to Suzanne's studio is ablaze with color in the fall. Dahlias and aster 'Alma Potschke' make this fall garden as appealing as it was in June.

mix of the plants, the architecture of the adjoining house, and any garden ornaments or structures. Of these three, the plants and architecture play the biggest roles. A gray-shingled Cape Cod house, a mix of hydrangeas, roses, and rhododendrons, and the quality of light that is found in the moisture-laden air near the shore all give Cape gardens their singular look.

Plants that are native to the region, such as American beach grass (*Ammophila breviligulata*), inkberry holly (*Ilex glabra*), and summersweet (*Clethra alnifolia*), contribute to an awareness of location. The way these plants are placed in

# Mixing It Up

Cape gardens are often a combination of annuals, perennials, grasses, and shrubs, and the palette of flowering shrubs and dwarf evergreens expands every year. Here are just a few of the many wonderful woody plants that can be combined with perennials and annuals in the landscape.

Yak rhododendrons (*R. yakushimanum*) and their cultivars are the answer to overgrown rhodies in gardens and foundation plantings. These dwarf rhododendrons have the same large, showy flowers that the full-sized shrubs do, but they grow only about 3 feet tall. Yaks grow best in well-amended soil and part shade.

'Lemon Drop' azalea (*Rhododendron* 'Lemon Drop') is a hybrid of the native swamp azalea (*R. viscosum)*, and, like that plant, 'Lemon Drop' is deciduous and highly fragrant. Because it blooms in July, when people are outside and can enjoy the fragrance, it is the perfect shrub to plant near a deck or patio or in a fragrance garden.

Magic carpet spirea (*Spiraea* × *bumalda* 'Magic Carpet') is the perfect tough, low-maintenance shrub for mixed-shrub gardens, perennial borders, or foundation plantings. Spireas tolerate drought, hot sun, and off-ocean winds, and 'Magic Carpet' has brilliant foliage color in addition to pink flowers. The leaves immerge a lime-yellow tinged with hot pink in the spring, grow to a light green in the summer, and turn to gold touched with red in the fall. Growing not quite 3 feet tall, 'Magic Carpet' is filled with pink flowers in June, and, if deadheaded as the blooms go by, the plant will continue to flower.

Vitex, or chastetree *(Vitex agnuscastus)*, resembles a late-season lilac or large-flowered buddleia when in bloom. This sizeable shrub (6 feet or taller) blooms on new growth, so its size can be controlled by severely pruning in the spring. It combines well in shrub borders with other large shrubs, such as forsythia, weigela, peegee hydrangeas, and rose of Sharon.

Spirea ogon (*Spiraea thunbergii* 'Ogon') would be an asset in the garden for its foliage alone. Finely textured, bright yellow leaves are the perfect contrast to plants with substantial green foliage and the ideal partner for anything purple. Sometimes labeled 'Mellow Yellow', this shrub is reputed to grow 4 feet tall and wide. Like all spireas, 'Ogon' is a carefree shrub, and, with its small white flowers in May, brilliant gold fall color, and reasonable size, it makes a perfect addition to the shrub border and perennial garden.

Old-fashioned weigelas *(Weigela florida)* were once suitable only for the largest gardens, and many of these first cultivars are still perfect for shrub borders or as specimen plants. But smaller varieties with varying leaf colors are now offered, so that a weigela is appropriate for any size garden. Just a few of the many wonderful varieties are 'Rubidor', with an eye-popping combination of yellow leaves and bright pink flowers, growing 5 to 7 feet high; 'Wine and Roses', which combines burgundy-purple leaves and pink flowers, growing 4 to 5 feet tall; 'Variegata Nana', which possesses pretty green-and-white foliage and light pink flowers, growing 4 feet tall; 'Midnight Wine', which combines purple leaves and dark pink flowers, growing only 2 feet high; and 'My Monet', the smallest of this group, which has variegated foliage and light pink flowers and grows only 12 to 18 inches.

Chardonnay Pearls deutzia (*Deutzia gracilis* 'Seward') is a lovely, compact shrub with bright yellow foliage. The white, pearllike buds open to small starshaped flowers in the spring, and the foliage adds color and texture all season. Growing 3 to 4 feet high and wide, this deutzia is perfect to mix in with annuals and perennials, or as a foreground plant in the mixed-shrub border.

Black lace *Sambucus (Sambucus nigra* 'Eva') offers finely cut, dark purple leaves and large pink flowers that resemble the blooms of Queen Anne's lace. This midsize shrub (4 to 6 feet) blooms on new growth, so it can be pruned in the spring if necessary. The foliage remains dark all summer, making it the perfect plant to add season-long color to the garden. Because the leaves resemble those of a Japanese maple, this plant can be used to add that look to a small garden where there isn't room for a tree. These purple leaves are particularly striking when placed next to plants with gold or blue foliage.

'Minuta' pine (*Pinus strobus* 'Minuta') is one of the many dwarf cultivars of the eastern white pine. This one forms a soft, round mound of bluish-green needles. The 'Minuta' pine grows 2 to 3 feet high and 3 to 4 wide, adding great texture and color to the garden.

Dwarf Hinoki false cypress (*Chamaecyparis obtusa* 'Nana') is one of the smallest Hinokis, growing very slowly to just 3 feet high. The dark, fan-shaped foliage is wind-tolerant and keeps its handsome color all year. Another cultivar, 'Nana Gracilis', grows in a pyramidal form to 6 feet tall. Hinokis do well in sun or part sun.

Gold mop false cypress (*Chamaecyparis pisifera* 'Gold Mop') is a shaggy, dwarf evergreen with relaxed, stringy yellow foliage. This small shrub has the best color when planted in full sun.

Russian cypress (*Microbiota decussata*) is a low-growing evergreen that thrives in sun or part shade. The branches are covered with ferny, bright green needles, and it grows only 12 inches high. The plant will grow quite wide, however, and the foliage turns a rusty color in the winter, returning to green in March. This plant is a good alternative to creeping junipers, which are prone to tip blight, especially when they are under irrigation.

Gordon Gaskill and Suzanne Sinaiko's memory lives on in Suzanne's garden, which is now owned by Suzanne's son, Jonathan Sinaiko, and his wife, Camille. The cottage-style perennial garden is maintained by two Provincetown gardeners, Mel and Polly Coté.

the landscape also defines the setting; a large group of informally planted beach plums (*Prunus maritima*) characterizes a
seaside garden as much as a neatly trimmed boxwood hedge
typifies a garden in England.

Nonnative plants that do well in a particular region may
also come to be associated with that area. Hydrangeas, for
example, are frequently linked to the Cape even though
they are not indigenous to the area. Ornamental grasses
that originated in other parts of the world are nonetheless
referred to as "beach grass," and several varieties of rambling
roses are commonly called "Cape Cod ramblers." Over time,

▲ It's the Fourth of July all summer in this herb garden at the entrance to the Hopkins House Bakery.

◄ At the edge of Jane Vollers's garden, a rustic horse waits to ride into imaginary sunsets.

when a plant does well and complements local landscapes, it becomes connected to that area in people's minds.

The way gardens are tended can also be specific to a region. In many parts of Europe, trees and shrubs are kept well pruned, partly so they fit in smaller spaces, and partly because this is the way that these gardens have been tended for hundreds of years. This manicured appearance is a classic look in that region. Plants on Cape Cod tend not to be

▲ Roses and hydrangeas in the front yard and the sweep of a tidal marsh beyond make this the quintessential summer cottage.

▶ Thomas Norton plants the pool garden with long, clean lines of summer annuals.

▶▶ These rambling roses bloom only once, but the owner of this cottage reports that they are *always* in bloom for the Fourth of July.

▲ A summer house anchors two long garden beds at the home of Larry and Beth Best. Thomas Norton, who plants and maintains the gardens, uses a combination of summer-flowering shrubs, perennials, and annuals, with a particular focus on plants with white flowers.

◀◀ A multitude of cobalt blue accents and flowering plants announces that summer *is* the season in this East Sandwich garden. When Jane Maio moved here in 1998, the yard was so overgrown that you couldn't see the house from the street. As an artist, Jane saw potential in the cottage-style house and the property, and after clearing out the unkempt plants and brush, Jane began to plant her garden.

◀ An espaliered pear tree adds charm to an otherwise bare area where there is no room for shrubbery.

as tightly controlled. In fact, the sea breeze is apt to create plants with an asymmetrical, windswept look, and this too contributes to a garden that looks as if it belongs near the shore.

To call attention to a garden's location, gardeners frequently choose to use ornaments that reinforce this sense of place. Lobster traps, boats, buoys, shells, clam baskets, light-houses, sea-worn stones, and images of maritime life are used in Cape gardens to complement the plants and emphasize the setting. But whether they are planted with native or exotic plants, and whether they are ornamented or not, Cape Cod gardens celebrate the sea that surrounds the area. The gardens and the people that tend them rejoice in this region by the sea.

Plants are perfectly positioned in the gardens at the Ampersand Guest House in Provincetown. The garden's designer, Robert C. Vetrick, not only has the right touch with roses, but also uses a talent for display in placing his collection of bonsai.

◀◀&▲ Grasses, hydrangeas, and a sculpture made of colorful buoys give this small garden its sense of place. Sheila McGuinness and Mike Wright's property does not have a lawn; the backyard is filled with a deck and a raised-bed cottage garden, and the fence provides an ideal place to display Mike's sculptures.

◀ A festive string of buoys decorates the McGuinness-Wright side yard, giving a seaside flair to the berry bushes and sunflowers.

Robert Vetrick's rose garden demonstrates how charming a small property can be. Dividing the garden into three levels makes it seem larger, and the vertical spaces, often overlooked in a garden, are used to their full potential.

▲ This garden is certainly lovely because of its layout and the flowers it contains, but any experienced gardener can tell that meticulous maintenance keeps it beautiful.

▶ The Provincetown sculptor and metalworker Michael Kacergis creates sculptures out of recycled metal objects, and his specialty is creating works with a nautical theme. These bells, now hanging from a seven-son flower tree (*Heptacodium miconioides*), were made from old gas canisters.

▲▶▶ The gray shingles and beach grass declare that this is Cape Cod, and the containers and casual deck furniture speak of the sea breeze and summer pleasures. For their Truro landscape David Kirchner and Scott Warner chose bright, summery colors, using blues and yellows in the containers and the deck chairs.

▶▶ Jane Vollers uses a single seashell as the focal point of this garden on the edge of an East Harwich woodland.

▶▶▶ It seems appropriate that the ornaments in a Cape Cod garden say something about the garden's location. Here 'Carefree Beauty' roses bloom and a clam basket on a post decorates the cottage garden.

Cape gardeners display lobster buoys in a variety of ways, but no matter where they are hung, their bright colors remind us to be grateful that we are by the ocean and that it is summer.

◄◄ The gardens at Bob McCandless's cottage colony have a sense of place *and* a sense of humor. Because the Four Gables Cottage Colony is pet-friendly, a fence is needed to protect the gardens. And what fencing material could be more appropriate than driftwood scrounged from the beach?

# INDEX

Page numbers given in *italics* refer to illustrations or material contained in their captions.